BLUE CHIP KIDS

BLUE CHIP KIDS

KIDS

WHAT EVERY CHILD (AND PARENT) SHOULD KNOW ABOUT MONEY, INVESTING, AND THE STOCK MARKET

David W. Bianchi

WILEY

Published by John Wiley & Sons, Inc., Hoboken, New Jersey.
Published simultaneously in Canada.

For general information on our other products and services or for technical support, please contact our Customer Care Department within the United States at (800) 762-2974, outside the United States at (317) 572-3993 or fax (317) 572-4002.

Wiley publishes in a variety of print and electronic formats and by print-on-demand. Some material included with standard print versions of this book may not be included in e-books or in print-on-demand. If this book refers to media such as a CD or DVD that is not included in the version you purchased, you may download this material at http://booksupport.wiley.com. For more information about Wiley products, visit www.wiley.com.

Library of Congress Cataloging-in-Publication Data:

Bianchi, David W., 1954–
   Blue chip kids : what every child (and parent) should know about money, investing, and the stock market / David W. Bianchi.
      1 online resource.
   Includes index.
   ISBN: 978-1-119-05719-2 (cloth); ISBN: 978-1-119-05856-4 (epdf); ISBN: 978-1-119-05855-7 (epub)
1. Finance, Personal–Juvenile literature.   2. Investments–Juvenile literature.   3. Money–Juvenile literature.
I. Title.
   HG179
   332.024–dc23

2015001111

Printed in the United States of America

10 9 8 7 6 5 4 3

To Bernard Darty
who provided the inspiration and encouragement for this book.

BLUE CHIP: one that is outstanding; top quality; an investment grade stock that is considered to be a safe investment based upon its past performance.

CONTENTS

PREFACE

Go try to find the smartest boy and smartest girl in a high school class and ask them some questions about money, investing, and the stock market. How much do you think they know about managing money; about buying and selling stocks and bonds; about currencies and exchange rates; about price/earnings (P/E) ratios or puts and calls; about different ways to make money; about credit and debit cards; market share and initial public offerings (IPOs); about compound interest and being long and short stocks; about taxes, options, and index funds; about mortgages and market cap, the Federal Reserve and the Securities and Exchange

Commission (SEC); about how to analyze a company; and on and on and on. I guarantee you they know hardly anything at all.

Schools are simply not doing enough to teach kids the financial skills they will need to thrive in the years to come. They are expected to learn it all someplace else. We are turning out "book smart" kids who know more by the age of 16 than prior generations ever knew at 21, but will they have the financial skills to manage the money they will earn, spend, and invest for the next 50 years? Who is teaching them about that? No one, as far as I can tell, and the research backs this up.

This subject matter does not have to be boring or intimidating or overly complicated. The basic principles are simple and, when presented with simple kid-friendly illustrations, the entire world of money, investing, and the stock market can be opened up to young people everywhere. And, if truth be known, parents will learn a lot too. As one person said, "Parents will buy this for their kids but secretly read it themselves; many adults don't know this subject matter either."

This book started out as a modest effort to "write a few pages" for our 13-year-old son, Trent, so that he would have some basic knowledge of money and investing. What I thought would be 10 pages or so turned into this: 100 topics with 165 illustrations drawn by Trent's high school cousin Kyle. The topics were written with Trent in mind, and that comes through as one reads the book. If you would like to learn more about these subjects, please visit www.bluechipkids.com.

Here we go. Let's take a journey together into the world of money, investing, and the stock market.

A NOTE TO THE READER

In writing this, it quickly became apparent that it was too confusing to always have to reference both males and females, "he and she," "him and her," every time there was a need to refer to a person. As a result, our editorial board, which consists of an equal number of "him and hers," decided that it would be easier to pick one or the other and stick with it throughout the book.

After a coin toss, monitored by a minister, a rabbi, and a priest, "heads" won and the decision was made to refer to everyone as a male. It was just the way the coin toss worked out and was not meant to suggest that males are any better at any of this than females; they are not. In fact, women may very well be better at it.

ACKNOWLEDGMENTS

The illustrations in this book were created by Kyle Bianchi (age 17) who is an amazingly talented artist. Each illustration was created by him based on e-mail descriptions from me. Kyle quickly grasped the concept for each image and produced exactly what was asked for and he did it all in record time. Thanks, Kyle. ☺

Finally, this book would not have been possible without the ongoing support and encouragement of my beautiful wife and Trent's devoted mother, Julia, who continues to spend all of her time trying to make the world a better place.

"BLUE CHIP KIDS, YOU ARE CLEARED
FOR TAKE OFF."

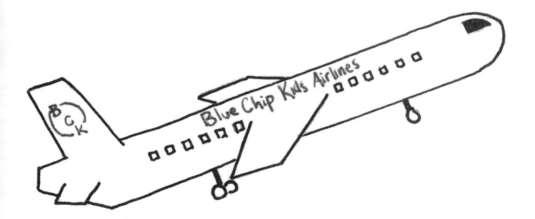

CHAPTER 1

MONEY, MONEY, MONEY

Money comes in all shapes, sizes, and colors. It flows around the world all day long, and thanks to computers you can even make it disappear with the push of a button.

The Journey Begins

You need money for everything these days.

You have to pay just to be born; you have to pay the hospital, you have to pay the doctor, you have to pay the nurses, and you have to pay for all the stuff they give you in the first minute of your life. Somebody gets a bill for all of that, and it's not cheap.

You have to pay to die. You have to pay the doctors and nurses who take care of you in the last minute of your life, and somebody has to pay for your funeral and burial after you are gone. That's not cheap either.

In between your first minute on this earth and your very last minute of life, you will need money for everything: food, clothing, a place to live, school, a car, insurance, vacations, the electric bill, the cable bill, your iPhone, your computer, gasoline, the lawn mower, furniture, your boat, presents for your family, and everything else you can think of. Money is as essential to life as we know it as oxygen is for breathing. Like it or not, you have to have money.

Over your lifetime you will earn money in a variety of different ways. You may start your own business, you may get hired by a company someplace, or you may trade stocks and bonds and make money that way. We don't know how you will make your money, but you will make money, and the thing you have to remember and never forget is: **You must live within your means.**

You need to save part of what you earn and not spend it all. You need to build up a bank account that has money in it to cover you when you are not making money or when unexpected expenses occur. It is imperative that you follow this rule.

Over the years I have seen far too many people create a lifestyle with all the trappings of wealth when they really could not afford it. They have huge houses, expensive cars, boats, and jewelry; they travel all of the time and spend money as fast as they make it.

LOAN DEPARTMENT

Even worse are the people who adjust their lifestyles to what their best year will finance. They may have made a lot of money in one year and then they go to the bank and borrow even more money to support a ridiculously extravagant lifestyle. Those are financial disasters just waiting to happen. Don't ever do that.

Live within your means. Spend your money wisely, and always remember to save money on a regular basis. Over time, you will be surprised by what you have put away.

Money in the bank will give you the security of knowing that you can weather whatever financial storm may come your way, and it will reduce the stress of paying for things.

You need to become a **disciplined saver** and a **conservative spender.** Live within your means.

Money from around the World—It's Not All the Same

Another name for money is **currency.** It's a different name for the same thing.

Most countries have their own currency. Some don't bother to create their own currency and simply use the currency of another country.

On the following pages you will see just some of the different currencies from around the world that are currently in circulation. They are colorful and attractive, and each depicts people or events that are important to that particular country.

The currency of the United States is the **dollar.** Everyone has seen a dollar bill. It is made from a special paper and is issued by the U.S. Treasury Department in Washington, DC.

The U.S. dollar is the most popular currency in the world. More international business is done with U.S. dollars than with any other currency in existence. Think about it; if a company in Japan manufactures a car and wants to sell it to a buyer in the United States, how should the Japanese manufacturer get paid? In dollars or in Japanese yen? Most international transactions like that are settled or paid for in U.S. dollars. Not all of them, but most of them. It is the most popular currency in the world.

What happens when a Chinese company sells clothing to a buyer in Japan? How should the Chinese manufacturer get paid? In Chinese yuan or Japanese yen? Or maybe U.S. dollars? The answer is, it depends. The buyer and the seller can decide between themselves how the manufacturer should get paid. They can choose any currency that they want to.

The point of all this is that there are hundreds of currencies in the world issued by hundreds of different countries, and people use them every day to buy things. There is no one global currency.

The Euro: What's That All About?

Although there is no single global currency, there are some regional currencies, that is, currencies used by groups of countries in certain parts of the world that have gotten together and agreed that they are better off using one common currency rather than a bunch of individual currencies.

The best example of a common currency is the **euro.** The euro derives its name from the word *European* for the obvious reason that it is a currency used by a group of mainly European countries.

The euro only came into existence in 1999 and was not really in use until 2002. It is a currency currently used by 19 countries in what is called the **Eurozone.** The countries in the Eurozone as of 2015 are:

1. Austria
2. Belgium
3. Cyprus
4. Estonia
5. Finland
6. France
7. Germany
8. Greece
9. Ireland
10. Italy
11. Latvia
12. Lithuania

13. Luxembourg
14. Malta
15. Netherlands
16. Portugal
17. Slovakia
18. Slovenia
19. Spain

Before the introduction of the euro, each of the countries in the Eurozone had its own currency. Austria had the schilling; Belgium had the franc; Cyprus had the pound; Estonia had the kroon; Finland had the markka; France had the franc; Germany had the Deutsche mark; Greece had the drachma; Ireland had the pound; Italy had the lira; Latvia had the lats; Lithuania had the litas; Luxembourg had the franc; Malta had the lira; the Netherlands had the Dutch guilder; Portugal had the escudo; Slovakia had the koruna; Slovenia had the tolar; and Spain had the peseta.

Every time you traveled from one of these countries into a different country, you would have to **convert** or **exchange** the money you had from one country into the currency of the country you were visiting so that you could buy things. It could be complicated at times and required a lot of thinking: You had to keep figuring out how much of the new currency you could buy with the currency you had from the other country. It was fun but complicated. With the euro you no longer need to do that. Now, you just use the euro in each of these countries and that's it. Simple.

To be clear, however, if you are using money from a **non-Eurozone** country you still have to go through the process of converting your money into the euro if you are traveling to a Eurozone country. If, for example, you have $100 U.S. and you are traveling to France and want to convert your money into euros, you will have to go to a bank or a currency exchange office, give them your $100 and they will give you euros equal to your $100.

The **exchange rate,** or how many euros they will give you for your $100, fluctuates all the time. As a result, what they will give you today is not necessarily what they will give you tomorrow.

There was a time when you could buy one euro for 90 cents U.S. Today it will cost you about $1.18. In other words, the euro has gotten more expensive or stronger relative to the U.S. dollar because you have to pay more for it today than you did when it cost 90 cents.

If the price of a euro would drop tomorrow back down to 90 cents, the euro will have weakened relative to the dollar and the dollar will have gotten stronger. Currencies are constantly moving up and down relative to one another, and those movements cause the exchange rate to change all of the time.

Establishment of the euro was controversial. Some people like it, and some people don't. It will more than likely survive as the common currency for these 19 countries, but the debate will go on as to whether it was or was not a good idea to have created it.

Exchange Rates and Currency Exchanges

If you live in the United States and want to buy a Toyota, what do you do? You go to the Toyota dealership, you select the car you want to buy, and you reach an agreement with the seller on the price.

Let's assume that the price of the Toyota you want is $25,000 including taxes, and let's further assume that you just happen to have $25,000 in cash in your pocket. You hand the dealer the cash, he gives you the keys to your new car, and off you go.

Now let's say you have a friend who lives in Canada and he wants to buy the exact same Toyota that you just bought. What does he do? Just like you, he goes to the Toyota dealership in Canada, selects the same car, and just like you agrees to pay with cash.

Your Canadian friend, however, is not going to pay with U.S. dollars. He is going to pay with Canadian dollars. As a result, he would have to pay $27,500 Canadian. How come? Why would he have to pay $27,500 Canadian when you only had to pay $25,000 U.S.? The answer: The U.S. dollar and the

Canadian dollar do *not* have the same value. One Canadian dollar is worth 10 percent less than a U.S. dollar. As a result, your Canadian friend has to use *more* Canadian dollars to buy the *exact same car.*

Comparing the value of the U.S. dollar to the value of the Canadian dollar is called the exchange rate. What can you get if you exchange $1 U.S. for Canadian currency of equal value? Or, the reverse, what can you get if you exchange $1 Canadian for U.S. currency of equal value?

Remember, at the time I am writing this, the Canadian dollar is worth 10 percent less than the U.S. dollar. As a result, if someone gave you one Canadian dollar he would only get 90 cents U.S. from you because $1 Canadian = 90 cents U.S.

Alternatively, if you gave $1 U.S. to a Canadian, he would have to give you $1.10 Canadian because one U.S. dollar is worth 10 percent more than one Canadian dollar. Get it?

The currencies of the various countries of the world are exchanged or traded every minute of every day of the year, and people make and lose money doing it all the time. But that is another story. At this point all you need to know is that the currencies issued by different countries have different values when compared to one another and those relative values go up and down all the time.

On the day that I am writing this, if you exchanged $1 U.S. for Mexican pesos, you would get 13 pesos. If you traded $1 U.S. for the Brazilian real, you would get 2 reals. If you traded $1 U.S. for the Colombian peso you would get—are you ready?—2,000 Colombian pesos. If you traded $1 U.S. for the Russian ruble you would get 35 rubles, and on and on and on.

You have been to airports where you see small kiosks where someone is sitting behind a glass window and you can exchange money with them.

All they are doing is taking the money you give them and giving you an equal value of whatever currency you want.

How does a currency exchange office know how much to give you? They know because they use their computer to look up the exchange rate on the **international currency exchanges** and then they add on a fee for their service. As a result, you are actually getting a little less than equal value when you give them your money, but that is the price you pay for the convenience of having a company employ the people who make the exchange for you. They have salaries and overhead to pay, and they need to make a profit for the service they are providing.

You can go to Bloomberg.com at any time, and you will find up-to-the-minute currency exchange information. There are other websites that do the same thing.

Different Ways to Make Money

There are many ways to make money. Here are just a few examples of different ways that people earn their living:

1. If your neighbor tells you he will pay you $10 to mow his lawn, you agree to do it for that amount, and he pays you the $10 when you are done, this is known as a **fee for service**.

In other words, you perform a single task, get paid for it, and you are done—a one-time fee for a one-time service. This is also known as a **fixed fee;** it is a payment, agreed to before the work begins, that is paid only after the work is completed.

2. You get hired to work at a company, and they agree to pay you $30 per hour. If you worked there for 40 hours per week (8 hours per day for five days per week) at the end of the week you would earn $1,200. This is a typical example of the **hourly wage** worker, and lots of people earn their living by being paid an hourly wage.

3. You could get hired by someone and paid an **annual salary** (i.e., an agreed-upon amount for working the entire year). Annual salaries are not dependent on the number of hours you work (although you are expected to work hard in order to keep the job). If, for example, your annual salary was $40,000, then each week you would be paid $769, which, over 52 weeks in the year, would add up to $40,000. $40,000 would be your **gross income** (a fancy name for **total income**) for the year.

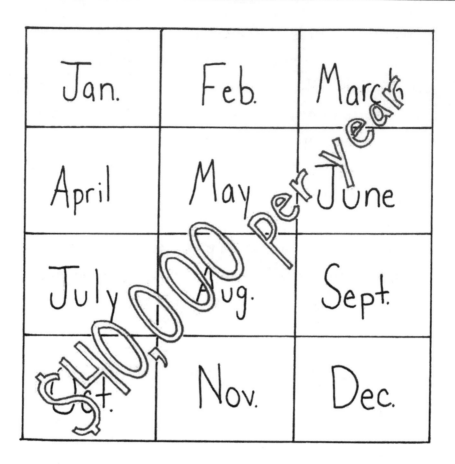

4. You could have a job where your income is not based on hourly wages or even an annual salary but, instead, on how much business you generate for the company each year. For example, you could be hired to sell all of the condos in a new high-rise building, and the developer might agree to pay you 5 percent of the total value of all of the condos that you sell for the company in one year.

Payments in this form are typically referred to as **commissions.** You are paid a commission or a **percentage of all of the sales that you generate.** If you sold $100 million in condos in one year, your commission, or gross income, would be 5 percent of $100 million, or

$5 million. If you sell nothing, you get paid nothing, but if you sell a lot, your income could be very big.

5. Another way to earn money is with a **contingent fee,** which is what a lot of lawyers do. It is similar to a commission system in the sense that you get paid only if you are successful and you get nothing if you lose.

   With a contingent fee, the lawyer gets hired by the client, works on the case for however long it takes to resolve, and then gets a contingent fee that is equal to an agreed–upon percentage of the client's recovery. In other words, the fee is contingent on the outcome of the case. No recovery for the client, no fee for the lawyer. If, for example, the lawyer settles the case for $100,000 and the lawyer's contingent fee is 30 percent of the recovery, then the lawyer's gross income for that case would be $30,000.

6. Many successful people earn their money not by being paid fees or wages but by starting a company, building up its value over time, and then **selling the business** for a lot of money years later. In these situations, the business owner typically makes all of his money when the company is sold and he "cashes out." This is happening a lot these days. Good examples include Google, Facebook, Twitter, and WhatsApp where the founders have sold all or part of their companies and become overnight billionaires.

7. Some people earn their money with a **combination of all these things.** Hedge fund managers are a good example of this.

Wealthy people will frequently invest some of their money in hedge funds. Hedge funds "hedge" their bets by investing in securities that supposedly make money regardless of whether the markets go up or down (it doesn't always work as planned and unsuccessful hedge funds close down all the time).

Hedge fund managers charge both a fixed fee and a contingent fee. The fixed fee is typically 2 percent of the money the investor invests in the fund. The additional contingent fee that is charged is, more often than not, 20 percent of the investor's profits. This is the so-called **2 and 20** rule. It is a way to make a lot of money if you are good at what you do.

8. **Consulting fees** are another way that people earn their money. Consultants are people who generally have an expertise in a certain area who get hired to offer advice to their clients on particular business matters.

Consultants typically charge a fixed fee plus reimbursement for their out-of-pocket expenses. For example, you could hire a marketing consultant for your new company whose job would be to meet with you and give you suggestions for how to grow your business, how to position yourself on the Web, how to get more customers, and so on. In return for his consulting advice, the consultant would be paid an agreed-upon fee plus reimbursement for his expenses.

9. Some people earn their money from **tips** or **gratuities** paid to them by people they take care of. The best example of this, of course, would be waiters and waitresses in restaurants.

Waiters and waitresses are usually paid very low hourly wages, but they get to keep the tips or gratuities that are paid to them by their customers. These payments are similar to a contingent fee and similar to a commission in the sense that they represent a percentage of their sales (usually 10 to 20 percent). Tips or gratuities have been around forever, and there are many people in our economy who are dependent on them for their annual income.

10. Another way to make money is by **trading things.** Someone has something that you want, you have something the other person wants, and the two of you agree to make a trade.

For example, a classic car dealer might agree to take your 1942 Rolls-Royce in exchange for a 1975 Ferrari that he has and that you have always wanted. You both believe you are getting a good deal, so you make the trade.

The car dealer subsequently sells the Rolls-Royce to a buyer he already had lined up, and he uses the money he gets from the sale to pay his bills. The house painter who can't afford to have his teeth fixed might say to the dentist that he will paint the dentist's house if the dentist will fix his teeth. They agree to the deal, and both end up with what they want.

People trade their way into acquiring goods or services without actually having to use cash all the time. The concept of trading one thing for another instead of using money goes back thousands of years.

Bitcoin

If you have been paying attention to the financial news lately you have probably heard all the talk about **bitcoin**. But what is that all about, and why would I even bother to mention it?

Bitcoins are a form of electronic currency allegedly created by Satoshi Nakamoto in 2009 along with a small group of private people in an attempt to establish a universal method for paying for things online without having to use conventional money.

Until now, currency as we know it has been created and issued by governments. It is backed by the **full faith and credit** of the issuing country, and it is accepted around the world as a legitimate form of paying for things. The bitcoin people want to change all of that and more and more businesses are now accepting bitcoins as payment for legitimate transactions.

Bitcoins, however, are considered by some people to be an unregulated payment process that invites the participation of criminals. In October 2013, for example, the U.S. Federal Bureau of Investigation (FBI) shut down the Silk Road, which was a bitcoin exchange service, and seized an estimated $23 million of bitcoins.

At this moment in time, the value of bitcoins is extremely volatile, and you should be very careful before spending any of your money buying them. I mention it, only to let you know that digital currencies may be here to stay and some time in your lifetime a new universal currency similar to bitcoin may be created, carefully regulated, and replace all of the currencies that we are familiar with today. Only time will tell.

CHAPTER 2

Different Ways to Pay for Things

It used to be simple: You buy something by paying cash. Now there are lots of choices: checks; credit and debit cards; online transfers; wire transfers; and now Apple Pay.

Checking Accounts

Your checking account is the account where the day-to-day management of your money takes place. It is the account where you deposit money that you receive either from your paycheck or someplace else, and it is the account from which you pay your bills.

Bills are frequently paid by writing a check to whoever has to be paid each month: Florida Power and Light for the electric bill; Miami-Dade Water and Sewer for the water bill; the lawn mower guy; the propane company for the propane you use for the stove and hot water tanks; the insurance company for your insurance policies; the air-conditioning repair company; the Visa and American Express bills; and so on.

Writing checks takes some time, but it is a good way to keep track of what you are spending. After a check is written, you make an entry in your **checkbook register,** which is a permanent record of whom you paid, the check number, the date you made the payment, and the amount of the payment.

Checkbook registers record payments made and deposits received: **money in; money out.** By carefully recording what you deposit and what you spend, you will know exactly how much money you have available to spend.

The following is a copy of a checkbook register:

■ AD-Automatic Deposit	■ AP-Automatic Payment	■ ATM-Teller Machine	■ DC-Debit Card	■ T-Tax Deductible	■ TT-Telephone Transfer		
NUMBER OR CODE	DATE	TRANSACTION DESCRIPTION	PAYMENT AMOUNT	✓	FEE	DEPOSIT AMOUNT	$ 10,800.00
1	7/2	Blue Chip Kids Airlines	400 —				9,600 —
2	7/3	Credit Card payment	600 —				9,000 —
3	7/7	Electric bill	300 —				8,700 —
4	7/8	Car Insurance	200 —				8,500 —
5	7/10	Lawn guy	100 —				8,400 —
	7/10	Deposit - pay check				700 —	9,100 —
	7/11	Wire transfer to E Trade	2,000 —				7,100 —
6	7/20	Rent	900 —				6,200 —
	7/22	Deposit - pay check				700 —	6,900 —
7	7/30	birthday gift card	200 —				6,700 —
8	8/1	Water bill	150 —				6,550 —
9	8/3	Deposit - dividend check				400 —	6,950 —

The money you have in your checking account is known as the account **balance.** It is the money that you have after you balance the deposits and the payments.

Once a month your bank will send you a **statement** showing you what deposits went into your account and what payments you made from the account in the previous month. It is then necessary to compare your checking account register with the monthly statement to make sure your records are correct. The process of comparing what you think you have with what the bank says you have is known as **reconciliation.**

You do not ever want to lose track of exactly how much money you have in your checking account. That is a sloppy way to conduct your financial affairs and can lead to an **over-draft** in your account—that is—writing checks for more money than you actually have. Should that happen, the check you write will be worthless and it is very embarrassing to give someone a worthless check. In addition, the bank will more than likely charge you an overdraft or penalty fee so your sloppiness will end up costing you money.

Electronic Bill Payment

Not too long ago there was no such thing as **electronic bill payment**. Now it is used all the time.

With electronic bill payment, rather than writing a check each month to pay your bills, you can use your computer to pay them. The computer allows you to transfer the money directly from your checking account to the account of who-ever you owe the money to. This is an increasingly popular way to pay bills.

You can also set up what is called **automatic electronic bill payment,** which is a system that will automatically pay your monthly bills directly from your checking account. Once you set it up, it requires no input from you at all other than making sure you have enough money in your account so that the bills can be paid.

For automatic electronic bill payment to work, you have to fill out a form with the company whose bill you want to pay each month—Florida Power and Light, for example— and once you fill out the form and give them the necessary information, they will make arrangements with your bank to have the money from your account automatically transferred to them on the first day of each month.

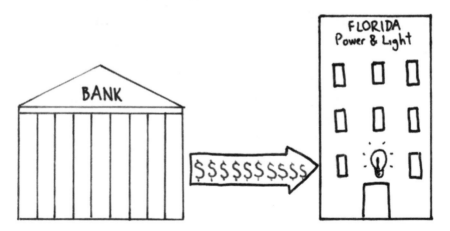

As a part of the electronic bill payment process, you can go online 24 hours a day, seven days a week and check your account to see precisely what bills have been paid and when the transfer of the funds took place. This online review allows you to see exactly what is going on. More and more people are paying bills this way rather than taking the time to write out checks, put them in an envelope, buy a stamp and then place them in the mail.

Electronic Banking

Electronic banking allows you to make deposits into your account or send money out of your account without having to personally go to the bank and make the transaction. You can do it all from your computer or your smartphone.

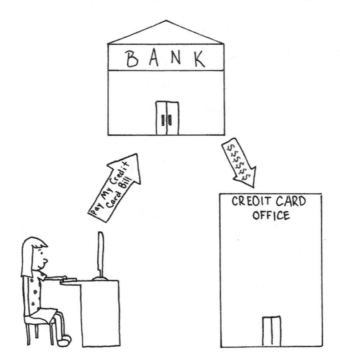

This has been a real transformation in the way banking is done, and it is a big time saver.

Credit Cards

Credit cards are issued by credit card companies and allow you to pay for things without having to use cash or a check.

The most popular credit cards in the United States are Visa, MasterCard, and American Express. These are publicly traded companies, and their stocks trade on the New York Stock Exchange (NYSE).

When you use your credit card to pay for something, the card is scanned at the point-of-sale, and two things happen in just a few seconds:

1. The computer checks to make sure your card is good and has not been cancelled for some reason.
2. A record of the sale is recorded on your credit card account. When that happens, you will get a bill for the purchase later in the month, and you can pay the bill either with a check or with electronic bill payment.

When you use a credit card, you are actually spending the credit card company's money until you pay your credit card bill. If, for example, you buy a washing machine for $400 with your Visa card on March 2 and you don't pay your credit card bill until April 2, you have had the benefit of using Visa's $400 for the 30 days before you actually paid for the purchase.

Think about how huge these numbers become when you consider all the people around the world who use credit cards every day. The credit card companies are advancing billions of dollars for purchases made by credit card customers before they ever collect payment for them. Despite this, however, credit cards are a very big source of revenue for the companies that issue them, and they are constantly trying to find ways to get as many people as possible to use them.

The credit card companies make their money by charging the store where you made the purchase a fee equal to approximately 2 to 3 percent of every credit card purchase. If, for example, you use Visa to pay for $100 of groceries at Whole Foods, the store receives $98 from Visa, and Visa keeps the remaining $2 as its fee.

When you add up all of the 2 percent charges that Visa and the other credit card companies receive for all of the credit card transactions that are made around the world every year, that is a huge source of revenue for the credit card companies.

Another big source of revenue for the credit card companies are the **finance charges** incurred by card users who do not pay their bills in full each month.

The customer's unpaid credit card balance immediately starts to incur interest at very high rates (12 percent or more) and the super-high interest that must be paid goes directly to the credit card companies.

Many people believe that credit cards are a win-win-win. The stores like them because they immediately get paid approximately 98 percent of what the customer just charged; the credit card companies like them because they are constantly collecting the transaction fees and finance charges that customers incur; and customers like them because they do not have to carry a lot of cash with them every day.

Another good thing about credit cards is that the credit card companies send the card users a statement each month showing them exactly what purchases they made. The monthly statements are a good way to keep track of your spending habits.

Apple has now moved into this business with what it calls Apple Pay, which is a way to use your Apple device to pay for retail purchases instead of using a credit card. It will soon be a very common way to pay for things.

Debit Cards

DEBIT CARD

Account Number: 16X30P49965
Card Holder: Blue Chip Kids
Expiration Date: 12/31/16

Debit cards look like credit cards, but there is a big difference: With debit cards, every time you use the card, the money is automatically **debited** or taken out of your checking account. If you don't have the money in your account at the time you use the card, then the transaction will be declined and you will not be allowed to make the purchase. That is not the case with credit cards. With credit cards, you can buy things even if you don't have the money in your account. You just have to have the money in your account when the credit card bill comes in at the end of the month so that you can pay the bill.

Debit cards are **pay as you go.** You are paying for your purchase with the money in your account the moment you use the card.

Wire Transfers

There are several ways to transfer money from one person to another: (1) hand the person the cash, (2) give the person a check, or (3) **wire transfer** the money into their account.

Transferring *by wire* is a term from the old days.

When you wanted to send cash to a person in another city you would go to a business like Western Union, and they would make the transfer for you. You would hand the clerk the cash you wanted to send, the clerk would send a signal on a telegraph wire to the Western Union office in the city where you wanted to send the money, and the clerk in that city would deliver the cash to whomever you told them to deliver it to. That process became known as a wire transfer.

Nowadays this is often referred to as an **electronic funds transfer.** It is simply a more modern way of transferring money from one person to another or from one bank account to another bank account. Despite the fact that it is now done electronically, it is still frequently referred to as a wire transfer.

CHAPTER 3

The Stock Market Is Cool

There are many stock markets in the world, and they all operate in a similar manner. As you read this, people are buying and selling stocks and money is being made and lost right now.

Stock Markets and Stock Exchanges: What Is the Difference?

A **stock market** and a **stock exchange** are the same thing. The terms are used interchangeably.

What Is a Stock Market?

A stock market is a place set up for the orderly buying and selling of stocks. That's it.

Think about it. If you owned 100 shares of Apple and there was no stock market, where would you go to sell your stock? You would have to start calling people to see if they wanted to buy your shares. That is not a very efficient way to make the sale. And, making matters worse, your potential buyer would not know what to pay you for the stock because he would not know what other people have been paying for it. It would be a mess.

The need for an orderly way to buy and sell stocks was apparent from America's earliest days.

On May 17, 1792, a group of 24 stockbrokers gathered under a Buttonwood tree on Wall Street in New York City and signed the **Buttonwood Agreement** establishing what would later become the **New York Stock Exchange (NYSE).** That was the birth of what is now America's oldest and most famous stock market.

Wall Street and the Stock Market

There really is a street in New York City called Wall Street. It is not a big street, but it is one of the most famous streets in the world. It is located in lower Manhattan in the heart of the U.S. financial district.

The world's biggest banks and stock trading firms have offices on or around Wall Street, and the NYSE is located there. The NYSE is what most people think of when they refer to the "stock market." You can go there if you want to and take a tour.

What you may not know is that there are lots of stock markets in the world, and there are even multiple stock markets right here in the United States. Here is just a partial list of some of world's most important stock markets where investors are buying and selling stocks and bonds, every day.

New York Stock Exchange (U.S.)

The NYSE has 2,308 listed stocks. It is the largest stock exchange in the world as measured by the total market capitalization (market cap) of the stocks traded there. Most of the biggest companies in the United States are traded on the NYSE, including AT&T, IBM, General Electric, General Motors, Ford, Caterpillar, Dow Chemical, Citigroup, Visa, Boeing, and Wells Fargo. If you want to buy or sell shares in any of these companies, your trade will take place on the NYSE.

NASDAQ (U.S.)

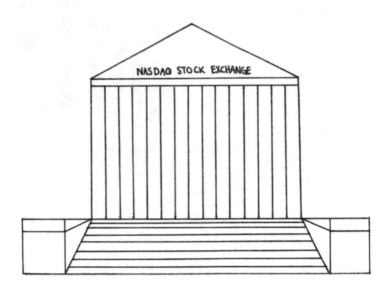

This is another very big U.S. stock exchange that is also located in New York City. It was started in 1971 and has 2,700 stocks listed and traded there. It is the second-largest stock exchange in the world. Some well-known companies that have their stocks listed and traded on the NASDAQ are Facebook, Microsoft, Twitter, Illumina, and Tesla.

The Tokyo Stock Exchange (Japan)

The Tokyo Stock Exchange is reportedly the third-largest stock exchange in the world as measured by the market cap of the 2,300 companies listed and traded there.

The London Stock Exchange (England)

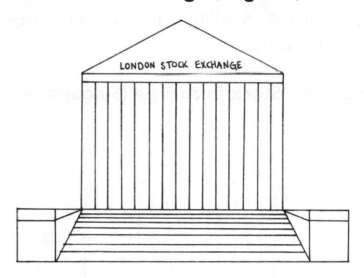

The London Stock Exchange was founded in 1801, and there are nearly 3,000 companies listed and traded on this exchange from 60 countries. It is reported to be the fourth-largest stock exchange in the world.

The Euronext Stock Exchange (Europe)

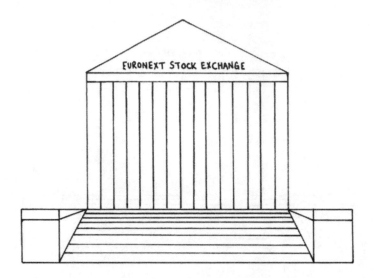

This is a European stock exchange with offices in London, Paris, Lisbon, Amsterdam, and Brussels. In 2007 it merged with the NYSE and is now known as the NYSE Euronext. It has 528 listed companies with a combined market cap of approximately $1.5 trillion. It is the fifth-largest stock exchange in the world.

The Singapore Stock Exchange (Singapore)

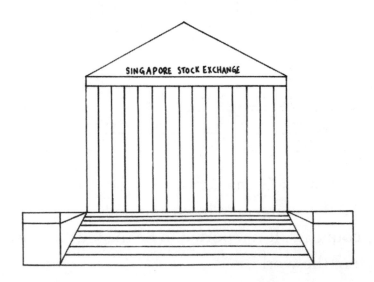

This one is relatively small but is located in an important part of the world. It was founded in 1999 and has about 800 companies listed and traded there.

The Sydney Stock Exchange (Australia)

This exchange traces its roots back to the mid–1800s. It is the eighth-largest exchange in the world and has 2,100 companies listed and traded there.

The Sao Paulo Stock Exchange (Brazil)

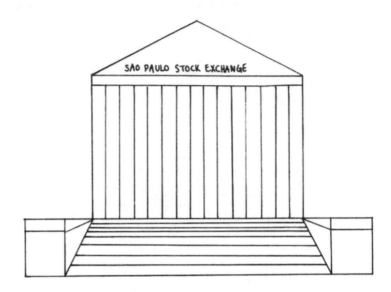

This is the thirteenth-largest stock exchange in the world and has 365 listed and traded companies.

Investor Stock Exchange (U.S.)

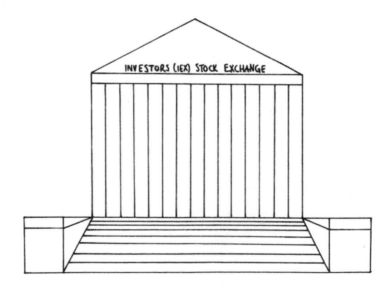

The Investor Stock Exchange (IEX) is new. It was started by various smart and wealthy people who wanted to find a way to trade stocks in a way that the high-frequency traders could not jump in front of them. We will look at high-frequency trading before we are done. At the moment only a very small percentage of the stocks traded in the United States get traded on the IEX, but this may grow over time.

These are just a few examples of the stock exchanges around the world. All in all, there are many stock exchanges in dozens of countries, and stocks are being traded every minute of every day someplace in the world.

Stocks

A stock is simply a piece of paper called a **stock certificate** that shows that you own part of the company that issued the stock to you. It is sometimes called a **security.**

If you own a single share of Google, for example, you are one of the owners of Google. If you own two shares of Apple, you are one of the owners of Apple. If you own three shares of Tesla, you are one of the owners of Tesla. Pretty cool, huh?

Let's say you start your own company called T.R.E.N.T. Inc., to manufacture and sell boats. At the time you form the company, you have to decide how many shares of stock you want the company to issue. It could be 1 share, 100 shares, 1 million shares or any other amount; it doesn't matter.

Since you are the only owner of the company, you make the decision that T.R.E.N.T. Inc., will issue 100 shares of stock. Take a look at what a stock certificate in T.R.E.N.T. Inc., would look like.

To carry this story a little further, let's pretend that someone comes along and decides that he likes the boats you are building so much that he wants to buy half your company. You are flattered. It is nice to know that people think enough of the company you started that they actually want to buy part of it. After thinking about it for a while, you tell him, "Okay, let's do it."

So... how do you sell half your company? It is simple. You own 100 percent of the company, and you have 100 shares. If you want to sell half the company, you have to sell the buyer half your shares (50 in this example). If you want to sell 25 percent of the company, you would have to sell 25 percent of your shares (25 in this example). If you want to sell 10 percent of the company, you would have to sell 10 percent of your shares (10 in this example), and so on. It's just math.

After you figure out how many shares you have to sell the buyer to give him the percentage of the company he wants to own, you then have to determine how much the buyer should pay for each of the shares. $100 each? $1,000 each? $1,000,000 each? You need to figure it out. Establishing a price for your stock is not easy.

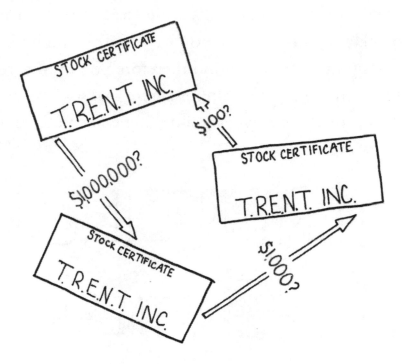

Let's assume that after your negotiations are completed you and the buyer agree on a price of $1,000 per share for each of the 50 shares he needs to buy in order to own half of T.R.E.N.T. Inc. As a result, the buyer gives you $50,000 (50 shares × $1,000/share = $50,000).

After the sale is completed, the number of shares that you own are reduced from 100 to 50, and the number of shares that your new partner now owns is 50 as well. The result? You each own half the company.

Hopefully the buyer turns out to be a good partner because he is now an **equal owner** of your boat company, and if the two of you have problems down the road, it will get messy very quickly. Neither one of you has control (you both own the same number of shares) and therefore you must agree on how to run things. If you cannot agree, that's when lawsuits get started, and that is never a good thing when you are trying to run a company.

T.R.E.N.T. INC.

WE'RE PARTNERS!

Never become partners with someone you don't trust and don't respect. It will lead to nothing but problems.

Stock Certificates

When you buy stock in a company you can receive a stock certificate evidencing the fact that you actually have an ownership interest in the company. A copy of a stock certificate follows.

Investors buy stock in companies all the time, but they almost never receive the actual stock certificate like they did years ago. How come? And how do they know that they actually own the stock if they do not receive the certificate?

These days the only thing that most investors receive evidencing their purchase of a stock is an online account confirmation with E*Trade or whatever brokerage firm they happen to use and they may also receive a confirming e-mail. But is that good enough? Should you be worried that maybe you don't really own the stocks you buy if you do not receive the actual stock certificates? Answer: no. That is the way it is now done. Very few people ever get the actual stock certificate anymore, and everything is now done electronically. It is the new normal.

Market Cap

What is the "value" of T.R.E.N.T. Inc., now that you just sold half the company to the new buyer? Here is one way to figure it out.

The buyer bought 50 shares of your company for $1,000/share, so he paid $50,000 for half the company. If half the company is valued at $50,000 then 100 percent of the company is valued at twice that much or $100,000 ($50,000 × 2 = $100,000).

The total value of all of the stock that shareholders own is called the **market cap,** which is short for market capitalization. In this example, the market cap of T.R.E.N.T. Inc., is $100,000, which is the value of all of the shares in the company (100 shares) multiplied by the value of each share ($1,000 per share).

$$100 \text{ shares} \times \$1,000 \text{ per share} = \$100,000 \text{ market cap}$$

Your new boat company has a value or market cap of $100,000. Not bad for a kid in seventh grade.

Bid/Ask/Spread

The price that the buyer is willing to pay for your stock is called the **bid.** If the buyer said to you, "I will pay you $700 for each of the 50 shares I want to buy," the $700 per share offer would be his bid. In other words, he is **bidding** or **offering** $700 per share for each share of your stock in order to try and get you to sell 50 shares.

If you think that price is too low and you want $1,200 per share, the $1,200 price you are seeking is called the **ask.** You are **asking** $1,200 per share.

The difference between the bid and the ask is called the **spread.** In this example the spread is:

$1,200 **ASK**

−$700 **BID**

_____

$500 **SPREAD**

You will see bid and ask numbers for stocks posted every day.

The basic economic principles for all of this are simple and universal: Buyers want to pay the lowest possible price when they buy something, and sellers want to receive the highest possible price when they sell something. This applies to the buying and selling of stocks just like it applies to the buying and selling of anything else.

The FREE MARKET
Determines the Price
of Everything

The Free Market and Valuation

How do we know what the value of anything is supposed to be in this world? How do we know that a BMW is worth $100,000 or that a gallon of milk is worth $4 or that an ounce of gold is worth $1,350 or that the price of a share of stock should be $241, or $100, or $10 or any other price for that matter? Why should one share of Apple be valued at $550 today and $600 tomorrow? Who says that's what the price should be at any given moment?

No law says that's what these valuations should be. President Obama doesn't set the prices. So who does?

The price of any asset in our economy is determined by the **free market.** The *free market* is the term that is used to describe the natural give and take between buyers and sellers who ultimately have to agree on a price where the seller agrees to sell and the buyer agrees to buy.

I want $100 for the watch I want to sell you. You only want to pay $50 for it. After we negotiate, we agree on a price of $75. And there you have it: The free market just determined the value of the watch.

This is exactly the same thing that happens in the stock market every day; buyers and sellers come together, negotiate on price, and make a deal. It is the same thing that happens on eBay. The free market is determining what the valuation or price is of all of the items sold on eBay each day.

When everyone is hot on Tesla, the price of Tesla stock shoots up because demand is high and supply is fixed; the number of shares remains the same, but more and more people are willing to pay more to get them. On the other hand, when everyone thinks a company like General Motors is in big trouble because of product defects, they want to sell the stock quickly and the price falls because they are willing to take less just to get rid of it. It is simple.

When Can You Buy and Sell Stocks?

The NYSE opens at 9:30 each morning and closes at 4 PM. You can buy and sell stocks at any time while the market is open. The NASDAQ has the same hours. After-hours trading is also available, but that is a story for another day.

Stock Market Indexes

As you know, there are 2,308 stocks traded every day on the NYSE and 2,700 stocks traded on the NASDAQ. The NYSE is a stock market, a place where people buy and sell stocks each day. The NASDAQ is also a stock market. These are two completely different stock markets with different companies listed on them.

What we will look at now is a way for investors to follow how those stock markets are performing. Did the NYSE go up or down yesterday? Same question for the NASDAQ: Did it go up or down yesterday?

How is anyone supposed to know how the **stock market** did yesterday when there are thousands of stocks listed on the exchanges? Some stocks did well, and some did not. As a result, when someone asks, "How did the **market** do yesterday?" the answer is, "It depends." What stock market are they referring to, and how do we determine the answer to that question?

When people ask about the market, they are usually referring to the NYSE since it is the oldest stock exchange in the United States and has many of the largest U.S. companies listed on it. Nevertheless, when answering, you need to be clear as to whether you are referring to the NYSE, the NASDAQ, or some other market.

We then get to the issue of "how do we know how the market did yesterday" since some stocks went up and some went down? Let's assume that you will answer the question by referring to the NYSE.

One way to get the answer would be to select a small group of stocks that are traded on the NYSE and put them into an **index** so that each day you can follow how that group (or index) performed. Did the index for the NYSE go up or down yesterday?

DOW PRICE MOVEMENT

Stock indexes really do exist, and they are watched very carefully by people who follow stocks. For the NYSE, there is the **Dow Jones Industrial Average,** which is the most famous stock index of them all. The **Dow,** or **Dow 30** as it is often called, is made up of 30 of the 2,308 stocks that are

traded on the NYSE. For the NASDAQ the index is called
the NASDAQ 100 and it is made up of 100 of the 2,700
stocks traded on the NASDAQ.

The 30 stocks that make up the Dow Jones Industrial
Average are:

1. (MMM) 3M
2. (AXP) American Express
3. (T) AT&T
4. (BA) Boeing Company
5. (CAT) Caterpillar
6. (CVX) Chevron
7. (CSCO) Cisco
8. (KO) Coca-Cola Company
9. (DD) DuPont
10. (XOM) ExxonMobil
11. (GE) General Electric
12. (GS) Goldman Sachs
13. (HD) Home Depot
14. (INTC) Intel
15. (IBM) International Business Machines
16. (JNJ) Johnson & Johnson
17. (JPM) JP Morgan Chase
18. (MCD) McDonald's
19. (MRK) Merck & Company Inc.
20. (MSFT) Microsoft Corporation
21. (NIKE) Nike
22. (PFE) Pfizer
23. (PG) Procter and Gamble
24. (TRV) Travelers Insurance

25. (UTX) United Technologies
26. (UNH) United Health Group
27. (VZ) Verizon Communications Corp.
28. (V) Visa
29. (WMT) Walmart
30. (DIS) Walt Disney Co.

In addition to the Dow and the NASDAQ 100, there are other well-known stock indexes as well. There is the **Russell 2000,** which is an index of not just 30 stocks like in the Dow but of 2,000 different stocks. The Russell focuses more on smaller companies, whereas the Dow is made up of much larger companies.

There is the **Standard & Poor's 500,** which is an index of 500 stocks, which makes it bigger and more representative than the 30 stocks in the Dow, but it is not as big and as broad based as the Russell 2000.

Investors follow the movement of these indexes very carefully, and you will hear how these indexes did each day on the evening news.

Initial Public Offerings (IPO)

The term **IPO** refers to an **initial public offering,** or the first time that a company offers its stock for sale to the general public.

Let's assume for the moment that you started a business in your garage to manufacture and sell glow-in-the-dark cases for iPhones. You make and sell a bunch of them, but you have spent your life savings getting the business going and you need more money to move into a real factory and hire some help. One way to raise the money would be to sell stock in your company to the general public and, if you did so, the first time you did that would be your company's initial public offering, or IPO.

Every year there are well-known companies that go public with an IPO. GoPro, Facebook, Twitter, and Tesla are good examples of companies that recently did that.

There are generally two reasons why companies want to do an IPO if they can:

1. By selling some of the company's stock to the general public (investors like you and me), the company will receive the money from the stock sale and then use it to expand the business and (hopefully) make it more profitable. It will be able to buy new equipment, build a new factory, hire more people, expand its sales and marketing efforts, buy new businesses, and so on. If it uses the money wisely, the

IPO can be very helpful. Companies need money to grow, and an IPO is one way to get the money.

2. The other reason companies like to do an IPO is that it gives the company founders, early investors, and employees a way to make some money. In the early days of a company the stock is in private hands and is **illiquid.** In other words, it is difficult to turn it in to cash because there is no real market to sell it.

By doing an IPO and becoming a public company, however, the privately held stock becomes **liquid,** and the shareholders who own it will have a place to sell some or all of their stock any time they want to. After years of hard work, it is a way for those who were with the company in the early days to monetize their investment. Many people have made a lot of money when their companies went public.

BLUE CHIP KIDS INC. IPO
STARTS TRADING TODAY!

Companies will frequently have big public relations campaigns in advance of their IPO to draw attention to the company and the upcoming stock sale. The company's chief executive officer (CEO) will appear on the financial news programs such as Bloomberg and CNBC and push to be interviewed by the *Wall Street Journal, Business Week,* and other financial publications. The result is often a feeding frenzy for the stock. Investors hear the company's story, like what the CEO is saying, and then go to E*Trade and other places and try to buy it.

When the price of an IPO shoots up rapidly on its opening day of trading, the company's employees and early stage investors can hardly contain their excitement. They are getting richer and richer with every uptick in the price of the stock, and they sit around all day calculating their increasing **net worth.**

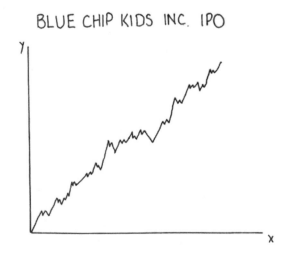

BLUE CHIP KIDS INC. IPO

"Let's see. I own 100,000 shares of my company's stock, and we just offered it for sale this morning at the IPO price of $40 per share, and all the stock we offered was sold out in

5 minutes. At 9:40 this morning I had a net worth of $4 million! Awesome! But now it's lunchtime, and the stock is trading at $60 per share; it's up $20 per share in only 3 hours, and my shares are now worth $6 million! Unbelievable! I just got $2 million richer in the past 3 hours! I love my company, and I love IPOs." But will it last? Is it an increase that is sustainable? Or was the hype overblown, and will this darling of Wall Street plunge back to earth just as quickly as it shot up?

This is exactly what happened with Facebook. Facebook was one of the hottest and most anticipated IPOs ever. Its IPO first started trading on May 18, 2012, and investors fought one another to buy shares. The initial offering price set by the company was $38 a share, and within hours the stock shot up to over $45 a share, an increase of 18 percent. But then the bubble burst. The IPO had been priced too high, and many investors immediately questioned the company's valuation.

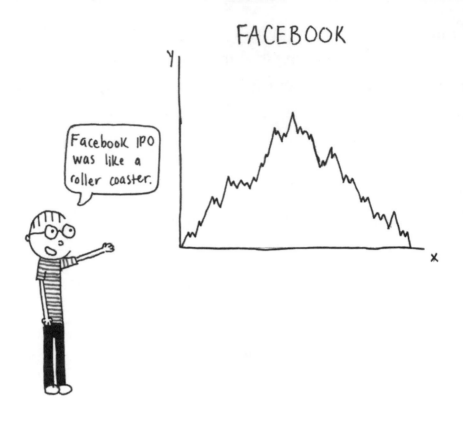

For a company that was not making any profits, Facebook had a **valuation,** or market cap, on the first day its IPO traded of nearly $120 billion, which was incredible. But those who bought the stock at $45 started selling and so did those who bought at $44 and $43 and $42 and $41. Even the investors who bought at $38 per share started selling. Investors got nervous and were heading for the exit. They wanted out of Facebook.

Within weeks Facebook's stock price had fallen to $27 a share, and all the investors who rushed to buy it when the IPO came out at $38 per share were not happy. Their euphoria had vanished and, on paper at least, they were watching their money disappear. Facebook has since rebounded and is now doing very well, but you never know. IPOs can go either way.

The Securities and Exchange Commission

The **Securities and Exchange Commission** is more commonly known as the **SEC.** It is an agency of the U.S. government that was created in 1934 to establish and enforce regulations pertaining to the buying and selling of stock, the operations of public companies, and related matters. Its job is to make sure that the investing public is protected from unscrupulous companies and stockbrokers who may want to mislead us in order to get us to buy their stock.

The SEC has the authority to investigate alleged violations of the securities laws, and it does so all the time. It can subpoena company records, pursue civil enforcement actions against companies and individuals who violate our securities laws, and it works with the Federal Bureau of Investigation (FBI), the Justice Department, and other enforcement agencies to assist in the pursuit of criminal charges against bad guys. In many respects the SEC is the sheriff of Wall Street.

Market Correction

A **market correction** refers to a big sell-off or downturn in the stock market, usually of 10 percent or more from the previous high. If the Dow had been at 16,000 and is now trading at 14,500 or below, many analysts would say we "are in a correction."

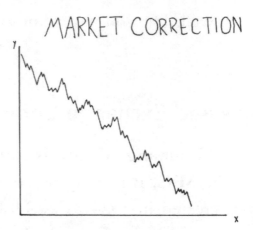

If the market has been red-hot and is at an all-time high, some on Wall Street will say, "We are due for a correction."

You will hear this term when you listen to the financial news programs.

Market Rally

A market rally is the *opposite* of a market correction. A **rally** simply means that stock prices are going up.

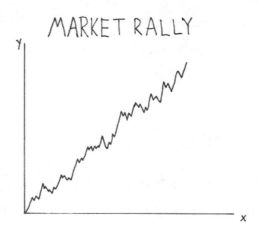

You will often hear people say that "stocks *rallied* today and the market was up 60 points." If you own stocks, the more rallies the better.

CHAPTER 4

Let's Buy and Sell Some Stocks

There is so much information available regarding the stock market, it is hard to know what to focus on. Here are just some of the terms that you should know about to have a better understanding of how it works.

Buy the Dips

This is a common expression you will hear when you listen to people talk about the stock market. **Buy the dips** refers to waiting to buy a stock until it has "dipped" or gone down so that you can buy it for less money than it is selling for now.

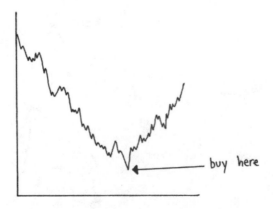

BUY ON "THE DIPS"

buy here

If you had a choice, would you want to buy a new bike for $400 or wait until it goes on sale and you could buy it for $300? If you waited until you could get it for $300, you would be buying the dip.

It is the same thing with stocks. Many traders will not buy stocks at today's price but will wait until there is a **market pullback** so they can buy the stock they want **on a dip.**

Bulls and Bears

If you look at the logo for Merrill Lynch, one of the nation's largest wealth management firms, you will see a drawing of a bull staring at you. Go ahead and Google "Merrill Lynch" and you will see what I am talking about. Why a bull? What is the significance of that?

In the world of money and finance, the bull symbolizes something that is strong, charging ahead and going up in value. If the stock market has been going up for a long time, people might say, "We are in a **bull market.**" If someone is asked where he thinks the market is headed in the months to come he might say, "I'm bullish on the market." In other words, he believes the stock market will continue going up.

The opposite of a bull market is a **bear market.** If the market has been going down for a long time some people will say, "We are in a bear market." If asked for an opinion on where the stock market is headed for the rest of this year, you might hear, "I'm bearish. I think it has more to fall before things get better."

Bulls and *bears*—are well-known Wall Street terms that reference opposite expressions for how the stock market or the economy are doing now or are likely to do in the future.

Paper Profits and Paper Losses

If you buy Apple stock at $525 per share and the price of the stock goes down to $400 per share, have you *lost* $125 per share? If you bought the stock at $525 per share and it shoots up to $650 per share, have you *made* $125 per share?

The answer to both of these questions is no. When you buy a stock and watch it go up or down *you haven't made money or lost money until you actually sell the stock.* That is when your gains and losses are determined. Until then, as the value of your stocks changes each day, you only have **paper profits** or **paper losses,** but that's it. By the way, your net worth changes each day as the value of your stocks goes up or down, but that is another story.

Risk On/Risk Off

When traders are moving their money out of the safety and security of cash or bonds and buying stocks in search of higher returns, those moves are said to be **risk on** trades. In other words, investors are willing to accept the greater risk and volatility of stocks and make riskier investments because they have greater confidence in where they think the stock market is going.

The converse of this is **risk off.** If investors are selling stocks, moving their money out of stock focused mutual funds and into the low-return but relative safety of cash or bonds, this is a risk off move. Investors who do this are worried about the direction of the stock market and the economy and have concluded that there is little likelihood that stocks will be going up any time soon. As a result, they sell their stocks and head for investments where there is little risk that they will lose their principal.

The ultimate risk off move would be selling out of stocks entirely and putting one's money in cash where the returns these days are less than 1 percent. Investors who do that are only concerned about protecting their money from loss and do not really care about what sort of a return they can get on the money. All they want to do is preserve their capital.

Stock Charts

There are people in the money management business who spend considerable time each week studying charts of historical stock prices and other financial indicators in order to determine the reasonableness of a current stock price. These people are called **chartists.**

By way of example, a chartist will look at a chart of Apple stock prices over the past year or 5 years or 10 years and try to determine whether there are any historical patterns to the movement of the stock that may (in his mind at least) repeat themselves going forward.

If the chartist notices that Apple's stock price trends up after it has been below its 52-week moving average and it is currently below its 52-week moving average, the chartist may conclude that it is getting ready to move up soon and he will buy it.

The same is true on the sell side. If the chartist concludes that every time Apple's stock trades at the upper end of its 52-week trading range it then falls by 5 percent, he may sell Apple before the price starts to fall again.

There are lots of different ways to use stock charts to try and get a sense for how a stock might move going forward, but sometimes what looks like a strong correlation between the movement of the stock's price and something else may just be a bizarre coincidence.

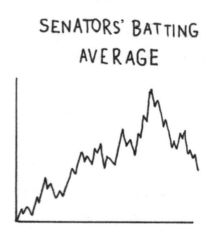

When I was in college I took an economics class where the professor put up a chart showing the historical price movement of the Dow Jones Industrial Average. He then put up another chart that looked almost identical to the first one.

Every time the Dow went up the other chart went up as well. Every time the Dow went down the other chart went down. It was remarkable. They were almost identical.

What our professor didn't tell us, however, was what the other chart was. After an hour of having us all guess, he finally told us. It was a chart of the batting average of the Washington Senators baseball team. Seriously.

The Washington Senators don't even exist anymore, but by some crazy coincidence the Dow Jones Industrial Average and the batting average of the Washington Senators baseball players moved in lockstep. If you were a "chartist" you might have concluded that if you could figure out how well the baseball team was going to be hitting in the next few days you would be able to predict how the stock market was going to move.

No one would have taken such a correlation seriously, but one could make the argument that "this is what the chart is telling me" (this is a favorite expression that chartists like to use). Be skeptical of this. The batting average of a baseball team is hardly a predictor of how the stock market is going to perform in the future.

Charts show historical data, and for that they can be very useful. They are suspect, however, if you try and use them to predict future stock price movements, and that is where you need to be very careful.

Market Top

As you look back on a chart of the stock market's performance (as reflected in the performance of the Dow, for example), you will see it move up and move down. There will be peaks and valleys and extended periods of troughs where it was at a low point.

A **market top** is the point on the chart where the stock market was at its highest, similar to this chart here.

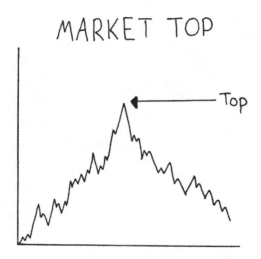

Market Bottom

The **market bottom** is just the opposite of the market top. It refers to the lowest point on a chart of the market's performance over a given period of time.

Ideally, investors would like to buy stocks at the market bottom and ride them up to a new market top, but it is too difficult to predict when that will occur. As they say, "you can't time the market." You just need to do your homework and buy good quality stocks when the prices seem reasonable.

Trading Range

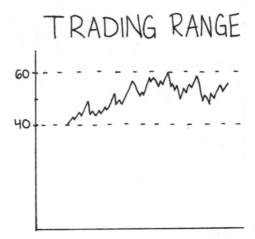

This is yet another common term when people discuss stocks. If, over the last year, the stock price of Coca-Cola ranged from a low of $60 per share to a high of $80 per share, the **trading range** for Coke was 60 to 80. If, over the last month, Coke traded between $75 per share and $80 per share, its trading range over the last month was 75 to 80. It is simple. Nothing complicated about it.

Being Long a Stock

If you watch the financial news programs you will hear people say they are "long Apple," or "long Facebook," or "long

Tesla," and so on. Being long a stock simply means that they own it. That's it. If you are **long** a stock, you own it.

Being Short a Stock

Some investors will **short** a stock, which means they sold a stock they did not own.

"Say what?!" They sold a stock they did not own? How is that possible? Imagine selling a bike to someone that you do not own, or selling a video game that you do not own. Who does that? Almost no one. But in the stock world, stocks are sold all the time by people who don't own them, and that process is called **selling short.**

People who sell stocks short **borrow the stock** from a stock brokerage firm and then sell it a few minutes later to someone else. As soon as they sell it they get to keep the money from the sale. How good is that? Well. . . maybe good, but maybe not so good.

When you borrow stock to sell it short, the day will come when you have to give the stock back to the person you borrowed it from. That date will be specified in the documents you have to sign when you borrow the stock.

If you sold the stock you borrowed, how can you return it to the person you borrowed it from? Isn't it gone the moment you sell it? Answer: Yes, it is. As a result, when it is time to return the stock, you have to go out and **buy the replacement shares** in the stock market and pay whatever the price happens to be at that time. That is what makes this trading strategy so *risky*. If you have to pay more to buy back the shares than what you received from selling them short, you will lose money on the trade.

Here's a quick example of how this works. Let's assume that Apple is trading at $500 per share, and you believe that things are not going well at the company. After doing some research you conclude that the price of Apple will go down over the next six months, and you decide to **short the stock.**

You contact a stockbroker, and he agrees to lend you 1,000 shares of Apple with the understanding that you have to give the stock back to him in six months. You agree. The broker then gives you the 1,000 shares of Apple, and you immediately sell them for $500 per share. Within minutes the $500,000 sale proceeds are deposited into your bank account (1,000 shares × $500 per share = $500,000).

Six months later you have to give the stock back, but you don't have it anymore because you sold it short. So what do you do? Answer: You have to buy 1,000 shares in the stock market regardless of the cost.

In our example here, let's assume that the price on the due date is $600 per share. This would not be good, because you will have to pay $600,000 to buy back the 1,000 shares. You sold them for $500,000, but you are buying them back for $600,000. You just lost $100,000 with your selling short trade.

Now let's look at what happens if the price of Apple went down to $400 per share over those six months rather than up to $600, as in the example we just looked at. Remember, you originally borrowed 1,000 shares of Apple and sold them for $500,000. If you buy them back six months later for $400,000 (1,000 shares at $400 per share) and then give the the shares back to the broker you borrowed them from, you will have made a $100,000 profit with your selling short trade. That would be a nice trade.

$$\boxed{\$100,000 \text{ profit!}}$$

When the price of the stock falls after you sell it short, you will make money. If it has gone up, you will lose money. That is the gamble. Will it go up or down after you short it? You can never know for sure.

High-Frequency Trading

High-frequency trading has received a lot of attention recently. It has been around for a long time, but it has existed in the shadows away from the glare of public scrutiny.

Everything changed in March 2014 with the publication of a book called *Flash Boys* by Michael Lewis and his subsequent interview on the television program *60 Minutes*. Lewis described in detail how high-frequency trading works, and a lot of people did not like what they heard.

Many people look at **high-frequency traders** as scalpers ripping off average investors and causing them to pay more for stocks than they would otherwise have to pay. Even Congress has gotten involved and is about to launch hearings into the whole thing. So what is it about high-frequency trading that has gotten everyone so worked up?

In a nutshell, high-frequency traders have set up trading offices with superpowerful computers, the most powerful routers and cable feeds that money can buy, and the fastest and most sophisticated algorithms on the planet. When the average investor attempts to buy Apple at \$525, for example, the high-frequency trader sees what you are trying to do and he speeds ahead of you to buy the stock before you do. You are then forced to buy the shares of Apple you want directly *from him* for a few cents *more* than you would have otherwise had to pay.

When high-frequency trading goes on with billions of shares of stock, the pennies add up and fortunes can be made with this trading technique. The profits that high-frequency traders are making come directly from the pockets of **investors** who are trying to buy stocks at market prices and have no idea that this is going on.

We don't know what is going to happen with high-frequency trading in the future. It is possible that the Securities and Exchange Commission (SEC) will ban it or at least regulate it in some way. Stay tuned for that. In the meantime, all you need to know is that this exists in case it comes up in conversations.

Fully Invested

Fully invested simply means that you have all your money invested in stocks, bonds, and other securities and you do not have any more cash to invest in anything. When that happens, you are said to be fully invested.

Leverage

Leverage refers to using something that you have such as money, influence, relationships, knowledge, and so on, to help you get something else that you want. For example, if you know a bunch of people on the City Commission, someone might say that you leveraged your relationships to get a zoning change. If you spent years studying how Medicare works and then started a successful business selling home health care to Medicare patients, someone might say you leveraged your knowledge of Medicare regulations to build your company.

NOT ALL "LEVERAGE" IS THE SAME

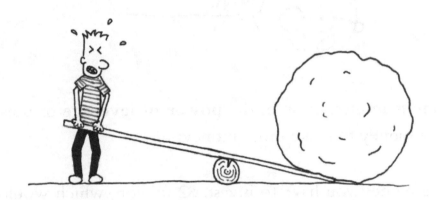

In the financial context *leverage* usually refers to using borrowed money to improve your returns on the money you have to invest. For example, if you expect to be able to double your money on what you invest in a deal, for every dollar that you can borrow you will be able to double the borrowed money as well. By making a profit on the borrowed money you will have leveraged the money you have into a better return on your investment.

Let's assume that you can buy shares in a start-up company for $1 per share and the company plans to raise $10 million by selling 10 million shares. If you have $2 million to invest, you will be able to buy 2 million shares or 20 percent of the company. If you have $3 million to invest, you will be able to buy 3 million shares or 30 percent of the company.

The only problem: You don't have $3 million; you only have $2 million.

Leverage can help you make even more money with your investments, but not always.

Here is an illustration of the **power of leverage** or borrowing money to make more money:

1. The money you have to invest: $2 million, which would allow you to buy 2 million shares, or 20 percent of the company.
2. Additional amount you will borrow to add to the amount to be invested: $1 million. You are leveraging the borrowed money hoping to make more money.
3. Total funds to invest with leverage: $3 million (your $2 million plus $1 million borrowed) for which you now get 3 million shares, or 30 percent of the company.
4. The company ultimately sells for $30 million.
5. You receive 30 percent of $30 million, or $9 million from the sale.
6. You then pay back the $1 million you borrowed and are left with $8 million. On your $2 million you ended up getting $8 million, which means that you quadrupled your money. It was a 4✗ return on your original $2 million investment.

If you had never borrowed the money (never leveraged your position) and bought only 20 percent of the company with your $2 million, you would have received 20 percent of $30 million when the company sold or $6 million. Thanks to leverage your net recovery from your $2 million investment was $8 million rather than $6 million. That is the power of leveraging. You were able to use the borrowed money to increase your profits by an extra $2 million. But be careful; if the investment did not work out, you would have to pay back the money you borrowed by dipping deeper into your savings.

CHAPTER 5

Stock Options

(Impress Your Friends with This One)

Don't be intimidated by this. It is really not that hard. You can buy and sell stock options just like you buy and sell stocks. They go up in value; they go down in value. Study this chapter and be the smartest kid in your class.

Options and the World of Puts and Calls

As you know, after you buy a stock its price can go up or down; you simply do not know what it will do despite how much research you may have done ahead of time or how confident you may be in your purchase.

To try to protect yourself from a big decline in the price of the stock you just bought, one thing that some investors do is buy and sell **options.**

There is a huge market out there where options are bought and sold every day. Just like stocks, you can follow the options market any time you want to on your home computer. Websites like Bloomberg.com, Etrade.com, and many others have options information available for you to look at any time you want to.

Options are cool, and if you spend a little time to understand how they work, you will know more than 99.9 percent of all the kids in the world about a very popular way to protect your stock investments and make money. So here we go; let's take a look at the world of options.

Options: How They Work

Options can be complicated, but the concept of how they work is not. There are basically two kinds of options: **puts and calls.** And every option is tied to a particular stock.

You can buy or sell puts and calls for Apple or Google or Coke or McDonald's or Disney or for almost any other stock you can think of, and here is why they are so cool:

- If you **buy a put** for Apple, for example, you can use it to force the person you bought the put from to buy your

Apple stock for *more* than you can sell it for in the open market.

- If you **bought a call** for Apple, you can force the person you bought the call from to sell you his Apple stock for *less* that what it would cost you to buy it in the open market.

How cool is that?

If you own the option, you are in control. Imagine selling something for more than it is worth anytime you want to! Or imagine buying something for less than what it is worth anytime you want to! In the world of Wall Street, it goes on every day.

Options Expire: They Don't Last Forever

Before we take a closer look at options, you need to know that options do not last forever. Just like a gallon of milk, they have an **expiration date** at which point they can no longer be exercised. Use them or lose them. You can buy options that expire in a few days or next week or even years from now, but all options have an expiration date.

Puts

Let's look at how puts work. Let's assume your bicycle is in good shape, but you have had it for a few years and want to get a new one. Before you can do that, however, you have to sell the old one. How do you do that? One way to do it would be to list it on eBay and sell it to the highest bidder. That would be a good way to do it. Let's also assume that after listing it on eBay the highest bid you get for your bike is $100. Should you sell?

What if there was another buyer out there and you could force him to pay you $120 for the bike? That's right. You could actually make him pay more than anyone else is willing to pay for it! Pretty good deal for you, right? You could make him buy your bike for 20 percent more than it is worth on the open market; 20 percent more than the best price you could get on eBay. It sounds awesome, so you do it.

How could you possibly force someone to buy your bike for more than it is worth? Answer: you could do it if you had bought a put option. In other words, if you had gone out and spent $10 to buy from Joe Smith a piece of paper called a put that would give you the right to force Joe to buy your bike any time you wanted him to for $120. You would have the legal right to put it to him whenever you wanted to; that's why it is called a put.

Why would Joe ever agree to this? Why would he agree to pay you more than the bike is worth? Answer: Because he received $10 when you bought the put from him. He wanted the money from the sale of the put, so he accepted the $10 and agreed to buy your bike for $120 if you wanted him to.

Joe was hoping that you would never come back; hoping you would never force him to buy your bike for $120. If you did, he knew he would have to buy it, but he was hoping that after he received the $10 that he would never hear from you again. Joe knew the risk that you might make him do this, but he was willing to take the risk so he could get the $10.

At the time, Joe looked at this as a really good deal for both of you. He made $10 by selling you the put, and you bought the protection and peace of mind of knowing that you could force him to buy your bike any time you wanted to for $120. You both thought it was a win–win.

More about Puts

Let's stick with the sale of your bike. When you forced Joe to buy your bike thanks to the $10 put option you bought from him, you exercised your option. In other words, you used the option that you had bought and forced Joe to buy the bike from you for $120. The $120 price Joe had to pay for your bike is called the **exercise price** or **strike price.**

So what did your bike actually cost Joe? $120? No. Remember, you paid him $10 when you bought the put from him several months ago, so Joe's real cost of the bike was the $120 he just paid *minus* the $10 he previously received from you, so his real cost was $110.

Joe's cost of the bike

$120 Joe paid for bike

−$10 Joe received for the put

$110 Joe's real cost of bike

Joe ended up paying $110 for a bike worth $100. It turned out that selling you the put just to get $10 wasn't such a great deal for him. You never want to pay more for something than it is really worth, and that is what happened to Joe because you exercised your put option.

For you, however, spending the $10 to buy the put turned out to be a good deal. By buying it you were able to sell your bike for more than it was worth on the open market.

How much did you actually receive for your bike? Simple, you received the $120 Joe had to pay you to buy it minus the $10 you paid to buy the put.

What you received for the sale of the bike

$120 received from Joe for the bike

−$10 you paid Joe for the put option

_____

$110 your net proceeds from the sale of your bike

By buying the put, you ended up **netting** $10 more than the $100 that the bike was worth on the open market. In this case, buying the option worked out well and allowed you to make some extra money, but that is not always the case. Sometimes options expire without having been exercised.

The Underwater Put Option (Say What?!)

What would have happened when it was time to sell your bike if you had found out that it was a collector's item and was worth $150 rather than the $100 you thought it was worth? Would you have exercised the put and forced Joe to buy it for $120? Not likely. Who would force a sale at $120 when you could go to eBay and sell it on the open market for $150? Nobody.

But what about the put you paid $10 for several months ago? What happens to that if you do not use it? Answer: When a put allows you to force someone to buy your bike at a price that is _less_ than it is really worth, you will not exercise the option; you will just **let it die** on the expiration date. Use it or lose it. If it is not used by the expiration date, it no longer has any value.

Options that you own allowing you to sell a stock for *less* than its current price (a put) or buy a stock for more than its current price (a call) will not be exercised by the expiration date and are said to be **underwater** and worth nothing. That's right: nothing, nada, zip, zero.

If the put you bought allows you to put the bike to Joe for $120 but the bike is really worth $150, you will not exercise it; it will expire without being used and will be worthless at that point. You will have spent the money for the put, but you will not use it. That is one of the risks you take when buying and selling options.

You may buy options but never use them.

But guess what? All is not lost because you can now sell your bike on eBay for $150, which is much more than you ever thought possible. Even after you subtract the cost of the $10 put that you bought and never used, you will still net $140 on the sale of the bike.

Your net proceeds from sale of bike

$150 received by selling bike on eBay

−$10 cost of put option that you never used
_____

$140 your net proceeds from sale of bike

Your $140 net recovery was pretty good. It was close to the $150 that this special collector's item bike was worth, and buying the put gave you the *peace of mind* of knowing that you could always force Joe to buy the bike from you for $120 if you wanted to. The $120 price became the floor on your sale price. By buying the put, you knew you would never do any worse than $120 when it came time to sell. That is the nice thing about buying a put option.

Calls

Let's change the story around for a moment. Let's assume that you don't own the bike we are talking about, but Joe owns it. And let's also assume that you really love his bike and want to buy it, but you don't have the money. You need to mow some more lawns and wash some more cars before you will have the money to get it.

"CALLS" are not phone calls!

In the meantime, while you are working to get the money, you are worried that Joe will sell the bike to someone else. So, what should you do? One of the things you can do is to **buy a call** option from him. By paying Joe some money you will have the right to **call** the bike away from him, that is, the right to force him to sell the bike to you at the price set forth in the option agreement. If you don't call the bike away from him by the expiration date, you will lose the right to do so and the call will expire.

BUYING A "CALL" OPTION FOR A BIKE

Let's assume that you and Joe agree that if you can get the money he will sell his fancy bike to you for $125. To make sure that you will be able to buy it at that price, you give Joe $15 for a call option; you are paying him $15 for the right to buy his bike for $125 at some point in the future. Joe immediately gets the $15 when you buy the call, and you get the peace of mind of knowing that as soon as you can earn $125 from your summer jobs the bike is yours if you want to buy it for $125 (i.e., if you want to **exercise the call**).

A month after you buy the call, you have finally earned the $125 to buy the bike. You then contact Joe and you exercise the call. You give him the $125, and he gives you the bike. You have successfully "called" the bike away from him.

So what did the bike actually cost you? $125? Answer: No. It cost you $125 *plus* the $15 you paid to buy the call from Joe. Therefore, the total cost of the bike to you was $125 + $15 = $140.

Your total cost for buying the bike

$15 paid for the call option
+$125 paid for the bike
_____

$140 total cost to you of the bike

I like buying CALLS because I know I never have to pay more than the exercise price stated in the CALL Option.

So, was it a good move to buy the call? Was it a good move to exercise the call and spend $125 on top of the $15 you already spent? Answer: It depends on how badly you wanted the bike and whether you could have bought the same kind of bike from someone else for less. If you really like the bike and could not buy it elsewhere for less than $140, then exercising the call was the right thing to do.

More about Calls

You buy call options when you think the price of the stock you are interested in owning may be going *up,* and you want to make sure that you can buy it at the call price and no more. The call price is known as the **exercise price** or **strike price.**

Let's use a real example. As I write this, you can buy Apple stock for $570 per share. You are thinking about buying it, but—for now at least—you want to use your money for something else. You are concerned, however, that Apple is coming out with some new products that will be big winners and the price of Apple stock will *likely go up* a lot. Should that happen, you won't be able to afford it. So what can you do? How can you make sure that you will be able to buy Apple at a price you can afford even if the price goes up to more than you can afford? Buying a call option may be the answer.

BUYING A "CALL" OPTION ON APPLE

If you could pay your friend Joe $25 to buy a call option from him that would allow you to call one share of Apple stock away from him for $570 per share any time within the next 90 days, would you do it? Probably so if you thought that the price of Apple was going to $600 or $625 or $650.

If you paid $25 for the call and then exercised the option at $570, your all-in price would be how much? Simple:

Price of the call: $25
Exercise price for Apple stock: $570
_____
Total or **all-in** price of the stock: $595

So … if you expect Apple to go to $600 or higher, then buying the $25 call would make sense.

The Underwater Call Option

Just like put options, call options can be underwater too; in other words, they can become worthless because it would make no sense to exercise them. In our example with Apple, if you paid $25 for a call that gave you the right to buy the stock from Joe (or call it away from him) for a price of $570, you would not bother to exercise the call if the price of Apple had dropped to $500. Right? Of course. It would make no sense to call the stock away from Joe for $570 if you can go to the open market and buy it for $500.

Under this circumstance, the call option that you paid $25 for is said to be underwater or worthless. You just have to watch it expire on its expiration date, and that's the end of it. You bought the call to protect yourself from having to pay too much for the stock, but you did not exercise it because it no longer had any value.

The Naked Call Option (OMG, Did You Say Naked?!)

If Joe sells you a call option for $25 that allows you to call the bike away from him for $100 but he doesn't have the bike when you bought the call, what happens? Under those circumstances, Joe sold you a **naked call option.**

When Joe sells you a naked call and you subsequently exercise the option and call the bike away, Joe has to go out, find the bike you want, and pay whatever it takes to get it. As the seller of the call option, he has the legal duty to make good on it. No matter what he has to spend, he has to find that bike, buy it, and deliver it to you for the $100.

This is a good example of why selling naked calls can be dangerous. The stock that the call relates to can get very expensive and you may end up having to spend a lot of money to go out and buy it and make good on what you agreed to deliver. *Be very careful* when selling a naked call.

Trading Options

A lot of people buy and sell options having no intention of ever actually exercising them. Instead, they buy them solely to try and sell them later for a profit. Options are traded (bought and sold) by investors all the time.

For example, if you buy a put on Apple stock for $25, you can go online and find out what that option is selling for any time you want to. If it has increased in value since you bought it, you can sell it for a profit if you want to long before the exercise date comes along.

Option prices go up and down all the time, and options trading is a big business.

The Chicago Board Options Exchange (CBOE) is the largest options trading exchange in the world. You can buy and sell options there on more than 2,000 different companies. You can learn more about the CBOE at www.cboe .com.

CHAPTER 6

FUNDS

(GIANT POOLS OF MONEY)

If you don't have time to do your own research on individual stocks you can invest in mutual funds, which are professionally managed, and your money is invested alongside many other investors. All you have to do is pick the right fund.

What Is a Fund?

A **fund** is a pool of money received from a large group of investors for the purpose of making investments in stocks or other securities.

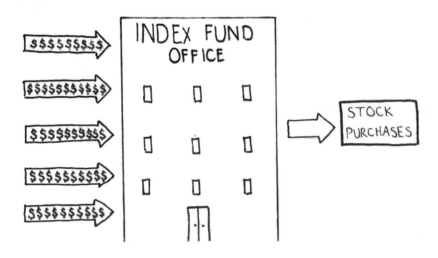

There are funds that focus on every kind of market sector that you can think of: high-yield debt funds; value funds; small cap funds; midcap funds; large cap funds; energy funds; real estate funds; technology funds; biotech funds; and on and on. Rather than trying to personally buy all of the stocks in those funds, all you have to do is buy shares in the fund of your choice, and the fund manager will make the stock purchases with the pooled money.

Index Funds

Some investors believe that the best way to make money in the stock market is to carefully research individual companies and buy stocks only in the most promising ones. Other investors believe it is too difficult to pick winning stocks that way and therefore you are better off buying an index fund. But what is an index fund?

An **index fund** is money pooled from lots of different investors that is then used to buy the exact stocks in a particular stock market index. The managers of the index funds do the work for you. You buy stock in the fund, and the fund in turn buys the stocks in the index that you want to invest in. It is simple.

If you wanted to invest in the Dow Jones Industrial Average, for example, how would you do that? Answer: You would have to go out and buy all 30 of the stocks that comprise the Dow. If you wanted to invest in the S&P 500, you could do that, too, if you bought all 500 of the stocks in the S&P. And you could even invest in the Russell 2000 if you had enough money to buy all 2,000 stocks in that index.

Index funds allow you to make investments in these well-known stock market indexes without having to take the time to personally select and invest in each of the stocks yourself.

Think of how difficult it would be to have to go out and buy each of the 2,000 stocks in the Russell 2000. It would take forever just to figure out what stocks are in that index. The same is true with the S&P. You would have to research the names of all 500 stocks in that index before you could even attempt to buy those stocks.

Index funds take the hassle out of the stock selecting and buying for you. The fund managers do the research and buying for you, and all you have to do is buy stock in the index fund itself. It is the easy and simple way to do it.

> INDEX FUNDS COPY
> THE STOCKS IN THE
> INDEX THEY TRACK

Index funds move up and down just like the value of any other stock you buy. When the Dow is up for the day, the value of your investment in the Dow Index Fund will be up for the day. When the Dow is down for the day, the value of your investment in the Dow Index Fund will have gone down for the day as well. Get it?

Index funds track the indexes themselves. That is the whole point. They are designed to move exactly like the indexes that they were created to reflect.

Mutual Funds

Mutual funds are a popular way to invest in the stock market and are very similar to index funds. There are more than 15,000 mutual funds in the United States.

As we saw, when you buy shares in an index fund, the fund managers use the money to buy the same stocks that mimic or copy the stocks in a particular index.

With mutual funds, you buy shares in the fund just as you do with an index fund, but the mutual fund managers are free to buy a much greater variety of stocks than the index fund managers are allowed to buy.

Mutual fund managers have very few restrictions on the stocks they can buy, and they are not trying to copy any particular index (if they were, it would be called an index fund). Mutual funds own a large basket of stocks, and you in turn own shares of stock in the mutual fund.

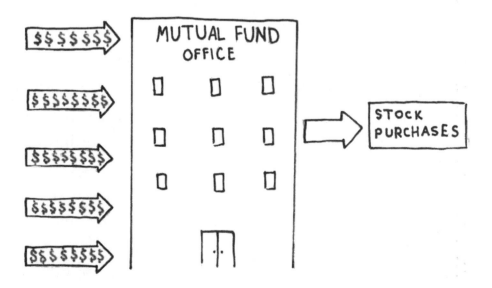

The *advantages* of a mutual fund are:

1. They are professionally managed.
2. They have great diversity because with all the money they have, they can buy shares of stock in many more companies than you can buy yourself thereby spreading your risk around.
3. They are regulated by the Securities and Exchange Commission (SEC) in order to protect the investors who buy their shares.

Some of the biggest mutual fund companies are Fidelity, Janus, Vanguard, Aberdeen, T. Rowe Price, American Funds, and Wells Fargo. Each has created many different mutual funds under its corporate umbrella, and each fund has its own symbol that you look up just like you look up a stock symbol. This allows you to follow the daily performance of any mutual fund that you are interested in.

When you study mutual funds you will see that these funds typically have a focus on something very specific. For example, there are lots of mutual funds that focus on **health care.** What does that mean? It means that if you buy shares in a health care mutual fund, you are investing in a fund that will take your money and use it to invest in companies that own hospitals, doctors' offices, health care clinics, health insurers, drug companies, laboratories, and so on.

If you buy shares in a mutual fund that focuses on the **energy** industry, you will be buying shares in a mutual fund that will use your money to buy shares of stock in oil companies, oil drilling companies, refineries, drilling equipment companies, pipeline companies, oil supply companies, and the like.

Take a moment and use your computer to look up the following **mutual fund symbols** so that you can see the type of information that is available regarding them. It is very similar to the information that is available for stocks.

ENBI
BIDL
DOWO
SOEN
SOPD

Mutual funds make their money by charging fees for what they do. You have to study their fee structure carefully to make sure you are not paying more than you think is reasonable.

Some typical mutual fund charges that you might have to pay whenever you buy a mutual fund include:

1. **Account maintenance fee**
2. **Front-end fees** sometimes known as **loads**
3. **Redemption fee** at the time you sell your shares back to the fund
4. **Exchange fee** when you move from one mutual fund to another

In short, mutual funds have all sorts of fees, and they will try to convince you in their advertising that their fees are lower than all the other mutual funds out there. Be very skeptical of such a claim, and do your homework before investing.

You can get all of the information you will need about mutual fund fees from the fund's website. There are also online companies that compare mutual funds and give you all the relevant information that you will need about them so that you can do a side-by-side comparison of fees, expenses, and historical performance. See www.morningstar.com for an example of one of the sites that provides that information for investors.

Hedge Funds

Hedge funds are similar to mutual funds in the sense that they pool money from many investors and then buy securities that they hope will go up in value so they can make a profit.

The big difference between a mutual fund and a hedge fund is that mutual funds generally limit their investments to stocks or bonds, whereas a hedge fund is free to invest in just about anything it wants to.

The hedge fund business is huge in the United States. By some estimates there is currently $2.4 trillion invested in hedge funds, and all of it comes from very wealthy people.

Before a hedge fund will even consider taking your money, you have to fill out a form and establish that you are an **accredited investor** and have a net worth large enough to absorb the loss of all of your money in the hedge fund in the event that the hedge fund investments fail. Hedge funds also have certain minimum investments, and more often than not, the minimums are well in excess of $1 million.

Hedge funds are operated by some of the smartest people in the financial industry who are attracted to that area because they can invest in just about anything they want to, and there is the chance for the hedge fund managers to make huge fees—and I'm talking *HUGE!*

The typical hedge fund charges each investor an annual management fee of 2 percent of the money under management. If, at the end of the first year, you had $1 million in your hedge fund account, your 2 percent fee would be $20,000. If, at the end of the second year, your account was up to $1.5 million, your management fee for the second year would be 2 percent of $1.5 million, or $30,000.

In addition to the annual 2 percent management fee, the hedge fund managers also charge a fee of 20 percent of all profits that they earn for you. If you gave them $1 million and in two years you sold your shares for a $2 million profit, you would pay an additional fee of 20 percent of the profit or $400,000 (20 percent × $2,000,000 profit = $400,000).

This is the so-called **2 and 20 fee structure** that we looked at earlier. You pay annual fees to the hedge fund of 2 percent of the funds in your account plus 20 percent of the profits that they earn for you. A lot of hedge fund managers have gotten very, very, very rich with this formula. Did I mention *very* rich? *Super* rich? Some of them make more than $100 million a year.

CHAPTER 7

BONDS AND CERTIFICATES OF DEPOSIT

(SOUNDS BORING BUT IT'S NOT)

Fixed income usually refers to the bond market. The bond market is bigger than the stock market and bonds are traded just like stocks are traded. So what should you buy? Stocks or bonds? Maybe both.

Bonds

A **bond** is another very common security or financial instrument. Unlike a stock certificate that evidences your ownership interest in a company, a bond is very different. A bond shows that you have lent money to the company and the company has to pay you back by the bond **maturity date.**

Let's say T.R.E.N.T. Inc., is doing so well with the 36-foot boat it manufactures that it decides to produce a 40-foot model. You are confident that if you can manufacture the 40-footers they will sell. There is only one problem: The company does not have the money to make them. You don't have the money to hire the designer for the new boats, you don't have the money to make the molds for the new boats, and you don't have the money to hire the employees to build the new boats. Where can the company get the money?

One way for the company to get the money is to sell bonds. After some careful analysis you determine that you need $1 million to produce the new boat. T.R.E.N.T. Inc., then offers $1 million of bonds to anyone who wants to buy them.

Each bond that the company sells has a **face value** of $1,000 and is **redeemable** in five years. In other words, each bond will cost the buyer $1,000 (the face amount), and whoever is holding the bond in five years will receive the $1,000 loan repayment (the redeemable part). Along the way T.R.E.N.T. Inc., will make annual interest payments to the bondholder.

The first investor comes along and buys ten $1,000 bonds for a total purchase price of $10,000. If we assume for the moment that the bonds pay interest of 8 percent per year, then every year for five years while the bondholder is waiting to get his $10,000 back, he will receive an interest payment of $800, which is equal to 8 percent of the $10,000. If the bondholder were to receive a 9 percent interest rate, he would receive an annual interest payment of $900 (9 percent × $10,000). If he were to receive a 10 percent interest rate, he would receive an annual interest payment of $1,000 (10 percent × $1,000).

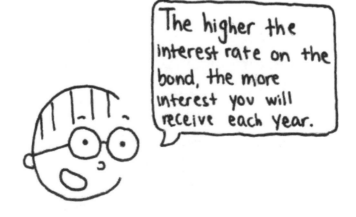

Interest payments to bondholders are a good way to receive annual income. If you own enough bonds and add up all of the interest payments that the bonds entitle you to receive, you can receive enough money each year to support your lifestyle. Many people believe, however, that when you invest you should buy a mix of stocks and bonds (known as a **balanced portfolio**). However, over the long run, history has shown that if you reinvest the dividends you own from stocks as you go, you will get a better return from owning stocks rather than bonds.

Yield

When you hear someone use the term **yield,** it usually refers to the annual rate of return an investor receives from owning a bond. For example, if you bought a $1,000 bond that pays 5 percent interest, the yield would be 5 percent, or $50, per year. If you owned a $10,000 bond that paid a 4 percent interest rate, the yield would be 4 percent, or $400.

A **high-yield bond** is a bond that pays a very high interest rate. They are sometimes known as **junk bonds.** Seriously, they are called junk bonds. But don't let the name fool you. Just because they are called junk bonds doesn't mean they are garbage and you should avoid them. If they are issued by good companies and you do your homework and are satisfied that the company will pay the interest and redeem the bond when it is due, then junk bonds can be good investments.

U.S. Treasury Notes and Bonds

Every week the U.S. government sells Treasury **notes** and Treasury **bonds** at an auction to raise money to pay for the ongoing operations of our government.

But what is the difference between a Treasury note and a Treasury bond? Answer: **duration.** Treasury notes have a maturity of 2 to 10 years from the date of issuance. Treasury bonds have a maturity of more than 10 years up to 30 years from date of issuance.

If you buy a two-year $1,000 Treasury note with a 3 percent interest rate, you are giving the U.S. Treasury Department $1,000, and the government is agreeing to pay you back the $1,000 at the end of two years together with 3 percent interest for each of the two years that you owned the note. In this example, you would receive a total of $60 in interest:

$1,000 × 3 percent interest = $30 of interest each year
$30 of interest per year × 2 years = $60 in total interest

If you buy a five-year $10,000 Treasury note with a 3 percent interest rate, the government will pay you back your

$10,000 at the end of five years together with interest of $300 per year for each of the five years that it had your money. In this example, you would receive a total of $1,500 in interest:

$10,000 × 3 percent interest = $300 of interest each year
$300 of interest per year × 5 years = $1,500 in total interest

If you buy a 10-year 4 percent Treasury note for $10,000, the government will pay you back your $10,000 at the end of 10 years together with interest of $400 per year for each of the 10 years that you owned the note. In this example, you would receive a total of $4,000 of interest:

$10,000 × 4 percent interest = $400 of interest each year
$400 of interest per year × 10 years = $4,000 in total interest

U.S. Treasury notes and bonds are commonly known as **treasuries,** and you will frequently hear the financial news commentators refer to the five-year U.S. Treasury note as the five-year and the 10-year U.S. Treasury note as the

10-year. There is even a **30-year Treasury bond,** which is the longest-duration bond issued by our government and it is often called the **long bond.**

The **10-year Treasury** is the most talked about Treasury issued by our government and is generally considered to be the **bellwether** for where interest rates are likely to move going forward.

Home mortgage rates are influenced by 10-year Treasury rates, and many observers of our economy will look to the current yield of the 10-year Treasury to get a sense for where mortgage rates are likely to go in the future.

People From Around The World Buy U.S. Treasuries

People from around the world buy U.S. Treasury notes and bonds because they are considered one of the safest investments in the world. They are backed by the full faith and credit of the U.S. government and, as a result, they have a *zero risk of default.* In other words, if you pay $10,000 for a five-year, you can be sure that at the end of five years you will get your $10,000 back when you go to redeem it, and you will get paid the interest you are owed along the way.

The U.S. government has never defaulted on its debt obligations in its 238-year history and it never will. As a result, many investors from countries that are less stable than the United States feel more comfortable investing in U.S. Treasuries than they do investing in bonds issued by their own countries. They sleep better at night knowing that no matter what happens in the world their U.S. Treasuries will continue to pay the interest they are required to pay, and they will be able to get their money back when it is time to redeem them.

One of the biggest buyers of U.S. Treasuries is ... you got it: China! The Chinese government buys more of our notes and bonds than any other foreign buyer in the world. That is why a lot of people say that the Chinese "own the United States," and if they stopped buying U.S. Treasuries, our government would not have the money it needs to operate. It is a sad reality.

What do you think would happen if the Chinese stopped buying our debt?

Basis Points

What's the basis for **basis points**? Is it some sort of way to keep score in a financial sporting event like, "Hey, I had more basis points than you did so I win?" Not exactly. Although it may sound like a big fancy term for some sophisticated financial score, it is nothing more than a term that refers to a fraction of a percentage point.

Let's say you have $1,000 in the bank, and the bank pays you 3 percent interest on the money. How much interest would you have at the end of one year? Answer: $30; 3 percent of $1,000 is $30.

Now let's assume the bank pays you 1 percent interest on your money. How much interest would you have at the end of one year? Answer: $10; 1 percent of $1,000 is $10.

But, what happens when you receive less than 1 percent on your money? What if the interest you are earning is one-quarter of 1 percent or half of 1 percent or something in between those two numbers? What is the interest on your money for something like that? To figure that out, you need to understand basis points.

Basis points are simply a fraction of 1 percent and to understand this term you need to know that 1 percent is equal to 100 basis points. Once you remember that, the rest is easy. To repeat: There are 100 basis points in 1 percent.

Since we know that there are 100 basis points in 1 percent then:

- 75 basis points equals 0.75 percent
- 50 basis points equals 0.5 percent
- 25 basis points equals 0.25 percent
- 10 basis points equals 0.10 percent
- 1 basis point equals .01 percent

A basis point is a fraction of 1 percent.

Basis points are referred to every day when discussing interest rates, and you will hear the term mentioned frequently when the financial news commentators talk about the **yield** on government bonds. For example, if the yield on a 10-year U.S. Treasury note is 2.87 percent and the next day the yield changes and is 2.90 percent, the yield went up 3 basis points. If the yield on the 10-year Treasury is 2.64 percent and the next day it drops to 2.54 percent the yield went down by 10 basis points.

Basis points are a way of tracking or describing the movement of interest rates when they move by something less than 1 percent. If an interest rate goes from 6 percent to 7 percent, it will be described as increasing by 1 percent, or 100 basis points. If it increased from 6 percent to 6.5 percent, it will be described as increasing by 0.5 percent, or 50 basis points.

Another way you will see this term used is if you borrow money from a bank. If you borrow $100,000, for example, the bank may say to you, "Your interest rate will be 50 basis points above the 10-year Treasury." So what does that mean? It means that if the 10-year U.S. Treasury note is trading at a yield of 2.87 percent on the day you close on your loan, then you will be charged an interest rate of 2.87 percent plus 50 basis points, which would be 3.37 percent.

Certificates of Deposit

Certificates of deposit are more commonly known as **CDs.** Let's say you have $10,000 that you will not need for living expenses anytime soon. You want to put the money someplace where it will be safe and earn some interest, but you do not want to make any sort of risky investment with it. One way to accomplish your objective is to go to a bank and buy a $10,000 CD.

A CD is a certificate that the bank will give you in exchange for your $10,000. The certificate will state how much money you gave them, how long you agree to keep your money at the bank (one to five years is a very common period of time), and it will state how much interest the bank agrees to pay you while you own the CD (these days the interest rate is about 3 percent).

CDs were particularly popular when interest rates were high, but interest rates are now very low and, as a result, people are not as willing to tie up their money for a year or more at a very low rate. Instead, many people prefer to keep their money in cash so that the money is available any time they want it for a higher yielding investment if one comes along. Nevertheless, CDs are out there, and you need to know that they exist.

If you buy a one-year CD with your $10,000, at the end of a year you will get your $10,000 back plus the interest. If the interest rate was 3 percent, at the end of the year you would get back $10,300.

The nice thing about a CD is that you are guaranteed to get your money back plus the interest. *There is no risk of loss.*

Unlike stocks and bonds, CDs are not traded and you cannot sell them like you sell stocks and bonds. The value of the CD is fixed and does not go up or down over time.

If, however, you should ever need your $10,000 before the year is up, you do have the right to **cash in** the CD before it is due, but you will be assessed a **penalty.** Should you do that, you might only get back $9,500, and you will not receive any interest for the period of time that you held the CD.

You need to keep this in mind if you decide to buy CDs. You never want to cash in a CD early if you can help it.

CHAPTER 8

Analyzing Companies
(Seriously, This Will Make You Very Smart)

Some people think you can throw darts at a list of stocks, buy the ones the darts land on, and you will do just fine. Other people believe you need to do your homework and dig deep into the details of a company. Here is what you need to think about if you want to really research a company before you buy its stock.

How to Analyze a Company to See If You Want to Buy Its Stock

How should you go about analyzing a company to see if you want to buy its stock? You like what the company sells; is that a good enough reason? That is one way. Other people are buying the stock? That is okay, too. You think they are about to become super successful selling their products and make lots of money? That's a good consideration. You have no clue but you think it is all dumb luck so you just buy anything and hope? There are people who do that, too.

The bottom line is that there is no right way or wrong way to decide how to buy a stock. There are as many different ways to make your stock-buying decisions as there are investors in the world. Having said that, however, you need to know a little about the basic considerations that many professional traders and wealth managers think about before they will buy a stock.

Some of the things that many people take into consideration before buying a stock are as follows:

1. *Price of the stock.* Is it high or low compared to where it has been over the past year?
2. *Price/earnings (P/E) ratio.* Is it reasonable? Is it more or less than the P/E on the Dow? If it is 10 to 15, that is fairly reasonable. If it is 50, that is crazy and you'd better have a really good reason to pay that much for a stock.

3. *Earnings history.* How many years has the company been making money? Have they been profitable each year? The longer, the better. Have annual earnings been growing over time, or have they remained flat?

4. *Market share.* Are they growing market share, or are they watching their competitors beat them out and take share from them?

5. *The overall market for their products.* Is the market for what they sell getting bigger or smaller? You want to buy companies that are in a market that is growing if you can.

6. *New technologies.* Are there new technologies that will make what this company sells less attractive to customers? Are there new technologies that will completely displace what this company does so that it is no longer relevant and just dies a slow death?

7. *Macroeconomic considerations.* Given your forecast for what is going on in the world in general, is that likely to help or hurt the company that you are thinking about buying? Is a war about to break out? Will oil supplies be disrupted? Will climate change impact the company?

8. *Breakup value.* If all else fails and the company runs into unforeseen problems, what is the intrinsic value of the company if they have to sell off assets to raise money? Are the assets and components of the business worth anything if they have to be sold off?

9. *Management.* This is perhaps the most important consideration. How good are the chief executive officer (CEO) and the people who run the company? Do they know what they are doing? Have they delivered good results

over the years? Are they in tune with what is happening in their industry? Do they care about the company?

10. *Is the company a takeover target?* One of the best ways for a stock price to go up is if another company comes along and tries to buy it. In a takeover attempt the acquirer almost always has to pay more than the current market price of the stock in order to buy the company. Is this company a takeover target?

11. *Intellectual property.* Does the company own any valuable patents or trademarks? These are also known as intellectual property. Patents can help protect a company from competition or at least make it more difficult for competitors to duplicate what the company is now selling in some reasonable period of time. Think of patents as a moat around a castle. The more you have, the wider and deeper the moat is and the harder it is for others to get at you. The same is true of trademarks. *Kleenex* is a trademark; *Coke* is a trademark; *Gatorade* is a trademark; *iPhone* is a trademark. All these terms are instantly recognized by consumers and add value to the companies that own them.

12. *Does the company pay a dividend?* Many investors will only buy stocks that pay a dividend so that they will have income to live on in the future. If dividends are important to you, then you need to look for stocks that have consistently paid them over the years.

These are just some of the considerations that professional wealth managers consider before they decide to buy a stock. You should think about them, too.

Price/Earnings (P/E) Ratio

When trying to decide what stocks to buy, one of the things to look at is a stock's **P/E ratio.** It is used by almost everyone in the financial world as one of the things to consider when analyzing a stock. So what is the P/E ratio, and how does it help you make a smart stock selection? Let's take a look.

The P/E ratio is the current price of a stock divided by the company's earnings or profits per share.

$$P/E = \text{Price of the stock/earnings per share}$$

To determine how this works, you need to know the following:

1. *The current price of the stock.* Let's assume that the current price of the stock is $20.
2. *The earnings* or profits of the company for the past year (earnings and profits are the same thing). Let's assume that the company had $1 million in earnings last year.
3. *The total number of shares* of the company's stock that are owned by shareholders. Let's assume that there are 1 million shares of the company's stock outstanding.
4. *The earnings per share* (EPS) for the company. This is easy. It is simply the company's earnings ($1 million in this example) divided by the total number of shares (1 million shares in this example). As a result, the earnings per share are $1.

Once you have this information, you can calculate the P/E ratio. Here's how:

1. *Determine the price per share.* That's easy. Just look it up on your computer to see what the stock is trading at that day. We are assuming a $20 stock price.

2. *Divide the price of the stock by the earnings per share.* In the example we are using here it would be:

$$\frac{P}{E} = \frac{\$20 \text{ (stock price)}}{\$1 \text{ (earnings per share)}} = 20$$

The P/E ratio for the stock in our example is **20.**

So why does this matter, and how can you use this information? It matters because knowing the P/E ratio allows you to get an idea of whether the price of the stock you are thinking of buying is cheap, expensive, or about right compared with other stocks out there.

This is really important, so let me repeat it. *A stock's P/E allows you to figure out if the price you have to pay for a particular stock is reasonable, cheap, or too high compared with other stocks.* It is one of the data points for a stock that you should always look at before deciding whether to buy it.

At the time I am writing this, most stocks traded on the NYSE have a P/E ratio of about 15. That means that, on average, investors are paying $15 (the price or "P") for each $1 of the company's earnings (the earnings or "E").

$$\frac{P}{E} = \frac{\$15 \text{ (price)}}{\$1 \text{ (earnings)}} = 15$$

If you are looking to buy a stock that has a P/E ratio of 35, you will be paying $35 for each $1 of the company's earnings per share. If you are considering a stock with a P/E ratio of 10, you will only have to pay $10 for each $1 of the company's earnings per share.

Buying a stock with a relatively high P/E or a relatively low P/E ratio is neither a good thing nor a bad thing. It is simply a data point. It is just one piece of information to look at when trying to decide whether the price you are being asked to pay for a stock is reasonable.

Having said that, however, if a stock you want to buy has a P/E ratio that is higher than 15 (which is the average P/E for stocks currently traded on the NYSE), you have to ask "why?" Why are people paying such a high price for this stock? What do they know that justifies such a high price, or is the current price just ridiculous?

Here are a few examples of some P/E ratios for real companies that are interesting. The data were accurate as of March 12, 2014:

1. Illumina (ILMN). This company makes machines that sequence DNA. P/E ratio: 82.
2. Wells Fargo (WFC). Wells Fargo is a big bank. P/E ratio: 12.
3. Tesla (TSLA). Tesla makes really cool electric cars. P/E ratio: 0. That's right: zero!

Ask yourself why someone would be willing to buy Illumina with a P/E ratio of 82 when he can buy Wells Fargo that has a P/E ratio of only 12. Doesn't it seem like a better deal to only pay $12 for every $1 of a company's earnings rather than $82? Think about it.

There are lots of smart investors out there who are buying ILMN with a P/E ratio of 82. What do they know about the company to make that super high P/E ratio and super high stock price seem reasonable to them?

Finally, look at Tesla. Its P/E ratio is 0. How can any company have a P/E ratio of 0? Answer: The company has no earnings at all. That's right; it is making and selling really cool cars, but it has not yet earned any profit. It loses money every day it is open. As a result, its earnings are zero and—by definition—its P/E ratio is therefore zero. *If a company has no earnings its P/E ratio will always be zero* because any stock price number divided by zero will always be zero.

The really amazing thing about Tesla, however, is that despite having no earnings (profits) at all on the day I am writing this, its stock price is $241 per share and the company has a market cap of $29 billion! (Remember: Market cap = total number of the company's shares × the price per share.)

Why do you think a company would be worth $29 billion when it has *no* profits? Answer: Investors think that sooner or later the company will be making lots of money and will be very successful. Should that happen, the price of the stock may go up even further and the current $241 price may look cheap. But maybe not. The investors buying at these levels may turn out to be very wrong.

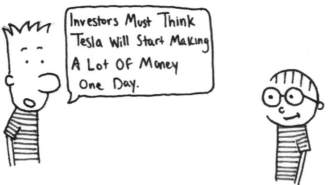

When it comes to P/E ratios, the good news is that you do not have to calculate a stock's P/E ratio on your own. The P/E ratio has already been calculated for you and is listed wherever you look up stock prices.

EBITDA

If you listen to CNBC or Bloomberg or if you read the financial newspapers, you will hear the term *EBITDA*. It is used all the time.

EBITDA is an accounting term, but we will not get into it in too much detail right now. All you need to know at this point is that it refers to a company's **E**arnings **B**efore **I**nterest **T**axes **D**epreciation and **A**mortization.

Someday you may take an accounting course, and at that time you will learn how companies maintain their financial books and records, how they record revenue and expenses, and how they determine what the company's profit is each year.

For now, just remember that EBITDA refers to the company's profit *before* the profit number gets reduced for things like interest payments, taxes the company has to pay, depreciation (that's a story for another day), and amortization.

Bottom line: From now on you can say: (1) "Yes, I've heard of EBITDA," and (2) when you are asked what it is you can say, "It has to do with determining what a company's profits are." That is good enough.

Market Share

This is another simple concept. Let's say there are two doughnut companies in the United States: Super Donuts and Mega

Donuts. If 1 million doughnuts are sold in the United States each year and Super Donuts sells 600,000 of them and Mega Donuts sells 400,000 of them, then Super Donuts has a 60 percent market share because it sells 60 percent of all the doughnuts sold in the country, and Mega Donuts has a 40 percent market share because it sells 40 percent of all of the doughnuts sold in the country.

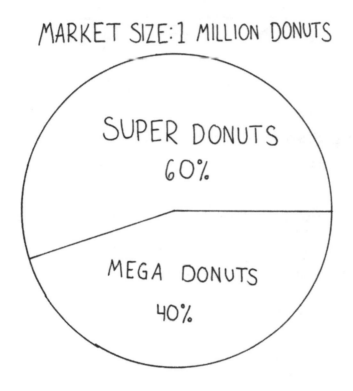

Let's pretend that for the current year, Mega Donuts is determined to win the doughnut battle with Super Donuts. The CEO of Mega is interviewed on TV and says, "We are totally focused on new and better doughnuts, and we are determined to take share from Super Donuts." Take what?! What does "take share" mean?

Taking share or **taking market share** means that Mega Donuts wants to take a bite out of Super Donut's 60 percent market share. Mega wants to sell more than 40 percent of the doughnuts in the United States this coming year, and if it succeeds, Mega's market share will grow. Should that happen, it will have taken share from Super.

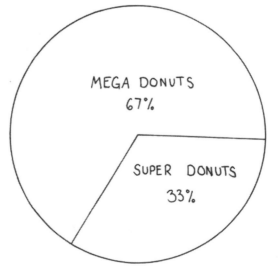

The size of the overall market for doughnuts, or any other product for that matter, is always 100 percent, so if Mega's percentage gets bigger, Super's must therefore get smaller. (We are assuming that there are no other doughnut companies in the country.)

If, next year, there are 1.5 million doughnuts sold in the United States, the size of the doughnut market in the country will have grown by 50 percent from the 1 million that were sold the year before. If Mega is now selling 67 percent of all the doughnuts in the country rather than just 40 percent that it used to sell, it will have taken share from Super Donuts in a larger and growing market for doughnuts.

That's all there is to it.

Earnings Season

Earnings season refers to the four times each year when publicly traded companies report their financial performance. These are known as **quarterly reports.**

The calendar year is divided into four quarters:

1. January through March is **Q1,** and that report is publicly released in April of each year.
2. April through June is **Q2,** and that report is publicly released in July of each year.
3. July through September is **Q3,** and that report is publicly released in October of each year.
4. October through December is **Q4,** and that report is publicly released in January of each year.

All publicly traded companies are required to report and release quarterly reports. Wall Street waits anxiously for the reports so that they can see how the companies are doing and whether they want to buy or sell the companies' stocks.

Over a two-week period most of the publicly traded companies release their quarterly reports, and this simultaneous release of all that information has become known as **earnings season.**

The release of the quarterly reports is typically followed by a conference call between company executives, Wall Street analysts, reporters, and some shareholders. The company discusses how it did in the last quarter and then answers questions that are asked by those on the call. One of the things that investors are really hoping to hear about in those calls is forward-looking guidance.

Guidance

A company's forecast of its future performance is known as **guidance.** You will frequently hear commentators say things like, "They have guided down for the rest of the year" (i.e., they are projecting lower sales and profits in the next few quarters), or the opposite, "They have issued guidance for improving sales and earnings going forward."

Guidance refers to a company's forecast for how it sees its business performing in the months to come.

Dividends

The objective of every company is to make money; the more, the better. When companies are making money, the value of the company's stock usually goes up and the employees and the investors are happy.

As companies make money they will often start to build up lots of cash, and the cash just sits in the bank until a decision is made about what to do with it. Much of it will be kept in reserve to help grow the company but many companies will use part of it to pay a **dividend** to the stockholders.

There are many companies that try to pay a dividend to their shareholders every year and are proud of the fact that they have done so every year for the past 20 years or more.

The dividend payments are anxiously awaited by the shareholders, and many of them rely on that money to pay for their living expenses. **Dividend-paying stocks** are popular, especially with older people who no longer work and use the dividends they receive as a form of wage replacement.

There is no set formula for how much a company will pay in dividends, but generally speaking, the dividend payments will be approximately 2 to 5 percent of the value of the company's stock.

If the company's stock is trading at $100 per share, you might see a dividend payment of $2 to $5 per share. If you owned 1,000 shares of stock, you would get a dividend check of $2,000 to $5,000 that year. It just depends on how much the company decides it wants to distribute to the shareholders and how many shares of stock you own.

Special Dividends

Sometimes companies will find themselves with an extraordinary one-time pile of cash due to a nonrecurring event that they do not expect to happen again. For example, they may have sold part of their business and received a large payment from the sale, or they may have just been piling up profits for many years. When that happens, the board of directors can decide to distribute the money to the shareholders with a one-time **special dividend.** It is special because it is not something that occurs regularly and is not something that the shareholders should expect to see on a regular basis in the future.

Stock Buybacks

Another option the board of directors has when the company has more cash than it will need is to launch a **stock buyback.** That is exactly what is happening with Apple as I write this.

In September 2013 Apple had $156 billion of cash in the bank. It was an extraordinary amount of money and probably a world record for any publicly traded company at any time in history.

The issue that Apple's board confronted was what to do with all of the cash. It was more than they needed to run the business, and as a result, many shareholders urged Apple to distribute the money to the the shareholders or otherwise use it to enhance shareholder value.

There were two ways Apple could do that:

1. A special dividend
2. A stock buyback

Apple decided to do both. It will distribute some of its cash with a special dividend, and it will start buying up its own stock that is traded every day on the stock market.

With stock buybacks, the price of the company's stock usually goes up because the **float,** or the number of shares of Apple stock available for the public to own, decreases. It decreases because the stock that the company purchases is retired and taken out of public circulation; it is no longer available for you and me to buy. As we know, stocks are ownership interests in a company, and when there are fewer and fewer shares owning the same very successful company, each share becomes more valuable.

If there are 10 million shares of stock in T.R.E.N.T. Inc., and each share of stock is worth $1, the value or market cap of the company is $10 million.

Now imagine that instead of having 10 million shares of stock in the company, because of your buyback there are only 1 million shares. Your company bought back 9 million shares, and they are no longer publicly traded. What happens to the price of the stock after that? Answer: It goes up.

T.R.E.N.T. Inc., is still the very same successful company it was before and is still worth $10 million as it was before. The difference, however, is that your stock buyback program reduced the number of shares in the company from 10 million to 1 million, and with only 1 million shares of stock outstanding, each share is now worth $10. The buyback program just increased the price of the stock from $1 per share to $10 per share, and the shareholders have big smiles on their faces.

Special dividends and share buybacks are two different ways to use a company's excess cash to increase shareholder value.

Transparency

Investors like to know what is going on with the companies they invest in. They are constantly looking for information about strategic planning, revenue and profits, the competition, forward guidance, and so on. If the company is not forthcoming with the information, you will hear many people say, "We need greater transparency with this company; we need more information."

Transparency simply means that the company needs to let investors have a clearer look at what is going on inside the company. The company needs to be more transparent.

Private versus Public Companies

This is pretty simple. A **private company** is one where none of the company's stock is traded on a public stock exchange like the NYSE or the NASDAQ. Private companies have stockholders just like public companies (they can have lots of them); it's just that shares of private companies are not traded on the public stock markets.

If you own stock in a private company, you can't go to E*Trade, for example, and look up the price of your stock like you can if you own Apple, Facebook, or McDonald's. Likewise, if you want to sell stock in a private company, you have the same issue. Since private company stock is not listed on any stock exchange, you can't just pick up the phone and tell your stockbroker, "Sell." Instead, you have to find your own buyer for a private transaction, and that can be difficult to do. As a result, private company stock is generally considered to be **illiquid** because there is no readily available market to sell it.

Public companies, on the other hand, are just that: public. Anyone in the world can own their stock simply by pushing some buttons on their home computer. Public companies frequently have thousands of stockholders and the stock is very **liquid.** You can buy or sell it any time you want to.

When a company makes the decision to **go public,** it does so with the understanding that it will be subject to lots of laws and financial regulations that it would otherwise not have to comply with if it were a private company. For example:

1. Public companies are listed on stock exchanges like the NYSE or the NASDAQ, and both of those exchanges have rules about what companies they will and will not agree to list. If your company does not comply with their rules, then it will not be listed and members of the public will not be able to buy or sell your stock on those exchanges.

2. Public companies have financial reporting requirements and must make their finances available for everyone to see. They have to file annual reports, hold an annual meeting of shareholders, allow stockholders to vote on who gets elected to the board of directors, sometimes vote to approve compensation packages for the CEO, vote to approve or reject the sale of the company to another company, and so on. Everything is so public with public companies that you can now sit at home with your computer and access more information about a public company than professional stockbrokers could have accessed just 20 years ago.

3. Public companies have to be very careful about what they say regarding their finances and how they are forecasting their future performance. If they tell the truth they are fine, but if they lie or exaggerate they can get into big trouble with the Securities and Exchange Commission (SEC). They can also be sued by both the government and individual shareholders. This happens frequently.

4. Some companies decide that the reporting requirements and public scrutiny of being public are just not worth it. When that happens investors with a lot of money can get together and **take the company private.** In other words, they can buy up all of the public stock, delist the company from the stock exchange, and go back to operating the business privately. The burdensome reporting requirements are then eliminated, but so is the public market for the stock. It is a two-edged sword. There are good things about going private, but there are downsides as well.

Private companies are also subject to various rules and regulations but not nearly as many as the public companies.

Shareholders in private companies have legal rights just like shareholders in public companies. They have the right to know what the company is doing, to see the financial statements of the company, to vote on certain things, and so on. The business of the company, however, is done privately, and the details of the company's business are not posted on the Internet for all the world to see. That is the big difference between a public company and a private company.

52-Week Moving Average

This is another common term, and as you get more familiar with the jargon of studying stocks you will run into it. The **52-week moving average** refers to the average price of a stock over the last 52 weeks. Every week the moving average changes because every week you are averaging a different group of 52 weeks.

To get the "moving average," throw out the oldest week and add-in the most recent week.

If the price of Google over the last year averaged $530 each week, the 52-week moving average for Google would have been $530. When you calculate the 52-week moving average next week, you would throw out the price from 52 weeks ago and add in this week's average price. With each week that goes by, you again throw out the oldest week and add to it the most recent week. By doing so, the 52-week moving average is always changing or moving.

Why is this important? Why do you need to know it? In and of itself it is not critical, but it is just another piece of information that is helpful in trying to determine whether the price you would have to pay for Google today is reasonable relative to where its price has been over the last year.

A **moving average** also shows you how the stock price has been trending. A chart of the 52-week moving average can tell you a lot about whether the stock is moving up or down. Like so many other pieces of information when buying or selling stocks, it is not critical; it is just another data point in your analysis.

CHAPTER 9

Borrowing Money

(Don't Borrow Too Much—Ever!)

There are many reasons why people borrow money, but you need to remember that it is often much easier to borrow money than to pay it back. Be very careful about taking on debt, or the burden of paying it off will get worse and worse.

Mortgages

Borrowing money to buy a house is probably the most common reason that people take on debt. There are two ways to buy a house:

1. You can pay cash for the house.
2. You can pay some cash and borrow the balance of the money from a bank.

When you borrow money to buy a house, the bank will get a mortgage on the property you are buying. So what is a mortgage?

A **mortgage** is a fancy term that refers to a piece of paper that the bank records in the county's property appraiser's office that lets everyone know that the house you just bought has been purchased with borrowed money. If someone wants to buy the house from you someday, the mortgage will have to be paid off before you (as the seller of the house) will get any of the sale proceeds.

Let's look at an example. Let's say you want to buy a house for $500,000. You only have $200,000 in cash, so you go to a bank and borrow $300,000 so you can make the purchase. Before the bank lends you the $300,000, however, you will have to sign a bunch of papers agreeing to pay the bank back—with interest—and allowing it to place a mortgage on your property.

As soon as you sign the papers and complete the purchase of the house, the bank will have its lawyers go to the county property appraiser's office and **record the mortgage.** Recording simply means that the bank's mortgage gets written or noted in the **official county property records,**

and anyone who wants to buy your property in the future will see it. A future buyer will not be able to buy your property until the mortgage gets paid off and the bank gets paid back. It is that simple.

When you have a mortgage, you will be required to make monthly payments to the bank to pay back what you borrowed along with the interest that is due. These monthly payments are due on a specific date, and you have to be sure that you make the payments on time. If you are late with your payments or stop paying altogether, you will be in **default** on your loan. As soon as that happens, the bank will start a **foreclosure** process to force the sale of your property so that it can try to recover its money.

In the example we are using here, if you failed to make payments on the $300,000 that you borrowed, the bank will foreclose and a court will order that your house be sold to the highest bidder. If the highest bid is $400,000, the house will be sold for that amount, the bank will take the $300,000 it is owed (plus interest), and you will get to keep what is left over (minus attorneys fees and related expenses).

If the highest bid, however, is only $250,000, the bank will keep all of the money from the foreclosure sale and you will still owe the remaining $50,000 of your original $300,000 loan. That is not a good situation to be in. You bought a house for $500,000 and ended up having it sold for a high bid of only $250,000.

You just lost the $200,000 that you put into buying the house, lost ownership of your house in the foreclosure sale, and have to move out *and* still owe the bank $50,000 from your original $300,000 loan. Very, very bad. You must always make your mortgage payments on time and never buy a house you cannot afford. *Remember the #1 rule: Live within your means.*

Amortization

Think about this. You just borrowed $300,000 to buy your house, and you know you have to pay the money back to the bank. But how much are you supposed to pay the bank each month, and for how many months are you supposed to make the payments?

Some home mortgage loans are paid off in 5 years, some in 15 years, and some in 30 years. It just depends on what the **terms** of your mortgage are.

Let's look at an example. If your $300,000 loan required you to pay the bank $1,000 per month every month until the loan was paid off, then you would need to pay $1,000 per month for 300 months before you would have the $300,000 paid off. Right? (I am leaving out the interest you would have to pay to keep this simple.)

If you had to pay the bank $2,000 per month, then you would have to pay that amount for 150 months before you would have the $300,000 paid off. If you had to pay the bank $100,000 per month on your $300,000 loan, then you would have to pay that amount for only three months before your mortgage would be paid off. Got it?

Amortization refers to the number of years you have to pay off your loan.

The process of determining how much you have to pay the bank each month in order for your loan to be paid off is called **amortizing** the loan. It is a fancy banking term for establishing how long you will have to pay off the loan and how much you will have to pay each month to pay the money back.

If you have 10 years to pay off the $300,000, then the bank will tell you that it will lend you $300,000 with a 10-year amortization. If you have 30 years to pay off the loan, the bank will tell you that it will lend you the money with a 30-year amortization. And so on. Got it?

Credit Ratings and Non–Real Estate Loans

Banks make all sorts of loans, but before they will lend any money, they do everything possible to make sure the loan will be repaid. We saw with real estate loans that banks will record a mortgage on the property so that they can force a sale if need be in order to get paid back.

But what can a bank do to protect itself when it makes other kinds of loans where the buyer has no real estate on which to record a mortgage? How does the bank make sure it is lending money only to borrowers who have both the ability and the willingness to repay the loan?

There is nothing that will absolutely, positively guarantee that any loan will be repaid, but one thing banks do before making any loan is to check the borrower's **credit rating,** and that is what we will look at now.

Let's assume two people walk into a bank and both want to borrow $50,000. The first guy, we will call him Jack, is 50 years old, is an executive vice president of General Motors, has worked at GM for 25 years, owns his own house with no mortgage on it, has never borrowed any money from anyone, and has an annual salary of $250,000. The second guy, we will call him Tom, is 25 years old, works at McDonald's for $9 per hour, has $75,000 in outstanding student loans, a $5,000 loan on his car, has worked in four different places in the last 12 months, and has no college education.

Who is the bank most likely to lend the money to and why? The answer is simple: There is a much higher probability that Jack will repay the loan. Tom is too big of a **credit risk.** As a result, Jack will get the loan and Tom may not.

Banks only lend money if they think you will pay them back.

Jack makes a lot more money than Tom, and Jack has no debt, so he is in a much better position to afford the monthly payments that will be required to repay the $50,000 loan. Tom, on the other hand, is struggling to get by. He is spending everything he makes and has no money in the bank to live off of if he loses his job. Jack is not a big risk for the bank, but Tom is.

The process of determining who is and is not a good credit risk is based in large part on a person's credit rating and in our example here, Jack had a much higher credit rating than Tom did.

A credit rating is like a score that you get on a school test. Some kids will get 100, some will get a 90, some will get a 60, and so on. Credit ratings work much the same way. Credit rating scores are based in large part on something called the

FICO score which was developed by the Fair Isaac Corporation, a company that used mathematical models to try and determine if a borrower is a good credit risk and likely to pay back his loan. FICO scores range from 300 (the worst) to 850 (the best).

With a school test, you can study and try to improve your score. Not so with your FICO score. FICO scores are given out by private companies, and you don't even know you are being graded. How crazy is that?

Believe it or not there are companies out there that are in the business of gathering all the financial information they can possibly find about you even though you have no idea they are doing it. They then give you a score, like your test score in school, and sell the data they have accumulated on you and the score they give you to banks and other companies that buy it from them. It is a huge industry.

The three **credit reporting agencies** in the United States are:

1. **Experian**
2. **Equifax**
3. **TransUnion**

These companies and others gather information on you in five different categories:

1. Payment history
2. Length of credit history
3. Amounts owed
4. Types of credit
5. New credit

Interestingly, how much money you make and your employment history are not factors in determining your FICO score although many lenders will look at that when deciding whether to approve a loan for you. A FICO score and being approved for a loan are two different things. A good FICO score does not necessarily mean your loan will be approved and, conversely, you may have a poor FICO score and still be approved for a loan if the bank is convinced that you will make your payments on time and pay off the loan when it is due.

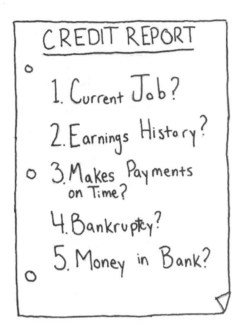

A **credit score** or **credit rating** will follow you around for many years. You might walk into Neiman Marcus, apply for one of the store's credit cards, and be told, "I'm sorry sir, but we cannot issue a Neiman Marcus credit card to you." Huh? How come? Why would they turn you down?

Stores frequently turn down customers for credit cards based on what they learn from the credit reporting agencies. The customer's credit report may have negative information on it, the FICO score may be bad, the customer may have too much debt, and so on. If they don't like what they see, you will not get a store credit card. It happens all the time.

Most people have never seen their credit reports, have never contacted a credit reporting agency to see what financial data has been accumulated about them, and have no idea what their FICO score is.

In today's world you need to pay attention to all of this. Federal law allows everyone in the United States to get one free copy of their credit report each year from each of the three nationwide credit reporting companies, and it is a good idea to see what is being reported about you. Often, the information in a person's credit report is wrong, and as a result, that person can be turned down for loans when he should not be.

There are many examples of people who have had to fight for years to get their inaccurate credit reports fixed, and there are now lawyers who specialize in nothing but fixing inaccurate credit reports for their clients.

Default

When something goes wrong in life, a lot of people start blaming others. Right? You've seen that before. They say, "Hey, don't blame me; it's default of him," or "It's default of her." Get it? (It's a joke.) Default, as in "the fault." But that's not what we're talking about in the world of money and finance when we use the word default. Let's take a look at what this term means.

Default simply means that someone who borrowed money fails to pay it back. That's it. If a city issued bonds to raise money to pay for new schools and it is unable to pay off the bondholders when the bonds are due, the city will have **defaulted** on the bonds.

If you borrow $100,000 from a bank and fail to pay it back, you are in default on your loan. If you fail to pay your rent on your office, you will be in default on your rent and will be kicked out. That's all there is to it. Default means that someone failed to pay back money that they owe.

Every time you lend money to someone, including every time you buy a bond (which is nothing more than making a loan to the person you buy the bond from), you have to ask yourself, "What is the risk of default if I make this loan?" In other words, "What is the likelihood that the borrower will fail to pay me back?"

If the risk of default is high, you should not make the loan or, at a minimum, you should insist on a very high interest rate to compensate you for the risk of default.

For borrowers who default, they may end up in bankruptcy, which can be a bad thing for the lender. Bankruptcy will frequently wipe out the debt to the lender and the borrowed money will never be repaid. Be very careful about whom you lend money to and avoid loans to people who have a bad credit rating and are at risk of defaulting.

Bankruptcy

Bankruptcy is a legal process by which you can attempt to have a federal bankruptcy court wipe out your debts so that you no longer have to pay back any of your loans. If the court allows you to proceed with your bankruptcy filing, when the process is completed you may no longer have to pay back any of the money you borrowed and you can then move on with your life with no debt.

That is the good news for someone who files for bankruptcy. *But there is a steep price to pay for anyone who declares bankruptcy.* Although you do get many of your debts wiped out and no longer have to pay back what you owe, once you declare bankruptcy it sticks with you for many years, and some debts cannot be discharged in bankruptcy at all.

After a bankruptcy filing it is very difficult to get anyone to lend you money. Many credit card companies will refuse to issue you a credit card (you will only be able to get a debit card). If you are a lawyer you have to report your bankruptcy filing to the state bar association. Whenever you fill out a financial statement in the future, you will have to answer "yes" to "Have you ever filed for bankruptcy?" You will be forced to sell almost all of your assets to pay back as much as you can to your creditors, and there will be big legal bills to pay for the lawyers to get you through the bankruptcy process. When it is all said and done, you will be broke by the time the bankruptcy process is over.

You should avoid bankruptcy at all costs. If you manage your money properly and *live within your means, you will hopefully never need to even think about bankruptcy.*

LIBOR

LIBOR is an acronym for **London Interbank Offered Rate.** It refers to the **interest rate** that banks in London would expect to pay if they had to borrow money from other banks.

The most common way that LIBOR is used in day-to-day business in the United States is when someone tries to borrow money from a bank. Banks will often quote the borrower an interest rate that is "2 points over LIBOR," or "1.5 points over LIBOR," or "3 points over LIBOR," and so on. The points they are referring to are percentage points. If LIBOR is 2 percent and you borrow money at 2 points over LIBOR, the interest rate on your loan will be 4 percent (LIBOR + 2 percent = 4 percent).

LIBOR is an interest rate that changes daily, and you can look it up on the Internet each day.

CHAPTER 10

Interest Rates

(Making Money While You Sleep)

Interest is the cost of using someone else's money. If you *borrow* money, you have to pay back the amount borrowed plus interest. If you *lend* money, you will get your money back plus interest.

Simple Interest

Simple interest is, indeed, very simple. If you lend someone $10,000 and you are to be paid 7 percent simple interest, you will receive $700 in interest payments for each year that the loan is outstanding.

If you make a five-year loan, for example, you will receive the following interest payments each year:

Year 1: $10,000 × 7 percent = $700
Year 2: $10,000 × 7 percent = $700
Year 3: $10,000 × 7 percent = $700
Year 4: $10,000 × 7 percent = $700
Year 5: $10,000 × 7 percent = $700
Total interest: $3,500

The question is: When does the $3,500 have to be paid?

Some loans require the borrower to make the $700 interest payments each year (or, alternatively, you may have to pay monthly, which would be $58.33 per month in this example). That is called **current interest.**

Other loans allow the borrower to defer or wait to make the interest payments until the end of the five years. In other words, the borrower pays no interest in years 1 to 5 but has to pay the full $3,500 all at one time when the $10,000 loan is due. That is called **accrued interest.**

If it is a simple interest loan, the borrower pays $3,500 regardless of when the interest payments have to be made. There is no extra money owed for waiting five years to make the $3,500 payment.

Such is not the case with compound interest. A 7 percent compound interest loan will cost the borrower more than $3,500. How can that be?

Compound Interest

Few things in the world of money and finance are more powerful than **compounding.** Never forget this. Repeat it over and over until it is burned into your brain: compounding, compounding, compounding.

As a lender, compounding takes your investment returns and turbocharges them. How? By giving you interest not just on the $10,000 you lent to the borrower but by requiring the borrower to pay you **interest on the unpaid interest** as well. In other words, the borrower has to pay *extra* for not paying all the annual interest that is owed each year. Watch how it works.

We start with the same $10,000 five-year loan you made to the borrower in our simple interest example. The interest rate remains the same at 7 percent, but this time we will compound it.

With compounding, the borrower starts out owing you the same $700 in interest at the end of year 1, but unlike our last example, he does not pay you at that time. Remember, in this example, he pays no interest until the end of year 5. The turbocharging starts in year 2 and continues each year after that for the life of the loan. Watch what a big difference it makes.

Year 1: **$10,000** × 7 percent = $700 in interest

Total owed by borrower after year 1: **$10,700.**

Year 2: **$10,700** × 7 percent = $749 in additional interest

(Interest for Year 2 is **$49 more** than in year 1.)
Total owed by borrower after year 2: **$11,449.**

Year 3: **$11,449** × 7 percent = $801 in additional interest

(Interest for Year 3 is **$101 more** than in year 1.)
Total owed by borrower after year 3: **$12,250.**

Year 4: **$12,250** × 7 percent = $857 in additional interest

(Interest for Year 4 is **$157 more** than in year 1.)
Total owed by borrower after year 4: **$13,107.**

Year 5: **$13,107** × 7 percent = $917 in additional interest

(Interest for Year 5 is **$217 more** than in year 1.)
Total principal and interest owed by borrower after year 5: **$14,024.**

Total interest borrower owes after five years when interest is compounded: **$4,024**

(Total simple interest owed in our last example was **$3,500.**)

As the lender, you have boosted your return with compounding by **$524 or 15 percent** ($4,024 is 15 percent more than $3,500). That is the secret of compounding. You are earning interest on the interest you are owed and making more money than you would earn if you lent the money at a simple interest rate. It's simple, and it is compounding while you sleep.

Annual Percentage Rate (APR)

When you see credit card ads on TV or other advertisements that contain financing terms for car sales, for example, you will hear about the cost to finance the purchase, the interest rate for the financing and the **APR,** or **annual percentage rate.** So what is APR? What is that all about?

To better understand APR, let's assume you want to borrow $10,000 from the bank and they will charge you a 5 percent interest rate. Is the cost of the loan to you $500 (i.e., 5 percent of $10,000)? Not necessarily, and that is where the annual percentage rate comes in.

In the documents you will have to sign to borrow the money from the bank, there will be a description of the fees and other charges that you will have to pay for the loan. In addition, you will find out if the interest is calculated at 5 percent for the year or whether it is calculated on a shorter period of time and compounded over the course of the year. In short, the APR is your all-in cost to finance or borrow the money.

There are laws in the United States that require the disclosure of the APR so that borrowers will know the true cost of borrowing money and will not be surprised by hidden charges when the bill arrives.

Disclosure of the APR also educates the borrower so that you can accurately compare the cost of borrowing from one lender (or car dealer, or credit card company) to another.

Got it?

CHAPTER 11

NET WORTH

(WHAT'S YOUR STUFF WORTH?)

Think of it as a thermometer that measures your money. As you work and save, your net worth will increase over time, and you can watch your wealth grow.

Assets

Assets are generally things that you own, such as real estate, jewelry, art, cars, boats, furniture, money, stocks, bonds, and so on.

Liabilities

Liabilities are generally things that you owe to other people such as any bank loans you may have, claims for money that others may have against you, legal judgments against you, ongoing payments that you have to make, unpaid taxes, and so on.

Net Worth

Net worth is a term that is used to determine the total value of all the assets that a person owns minus all of the debts and other things that the person owes to other people. In short, it is assets minus liabilities.

When someone says that Bill Gates is a billionaire, they are really saying that his net worth is more than $1 billion. If someone's net worth is $100,000, the total value of everything that person owns, minus all of his liabilities, is $100,000.

Here is a simple example to calculate a person's net worth:

Assets:
Market value of house: $250,000
Cash in the bank: $10,000
Value of stuff in the house: $2,000
Value of car: $5,000
Total value of all assets: **$267,000**

Liabilities:
Mortgage on house: $100,000
Credit card debt $20,000
Unpaid child support $5,000
Total value of all liabilities: **$125,000**

Net Worth:

$$\begin{array}{r}
\$267,000 \\
-\$125,000 \\
\hline
\mathbf{\$142,000}
\end{array}$$

Financial Statements

Financial statements are documents that you frequently have to submit to a bank when you want to borrow money. They are typically a page or two and set forth your assets and liabilities as well as a calculation of your **net worth.** They are signed by the person borrowing the money and are submitted under oath. In other words, you are swearing to the truth of what you have filled out. If you lied about what you have represented on the statement, you could face legal troubles and could even face criminal charges. Bottom line: Always tell the truth when you fill out a financial statement.

A sample financial statement form follows. Take a look at it and you will see how detailed they can be.

PERSONAL FINANCIAL STATEMENT

The following is my/our statement of all assets and liabilities as of the _____ day of _____, _____.

Applicant Personal Information		Joint Owner of Assets	
Name:		Name:	
Social Security #:	Date of Birth:	Social Security #:	Date of Birth:
Residence Address:		Residence Address:	
City, State & Zip:		City, State & Zip:	
Position or Occupation:		Position or Occupation:	
Business Address:		Business Address:	
City, State & Zip:		City, State & Zip:	
Res. Phone:	Bus. Phone:	Res. Phone:	Bus. Phone:

STATEMENT OF FINANCIAL CONDITION

ASSETS SOLELY OWNED (List here only those assets not jointly owned)	In Dollars (Omit Cents)	ALL LIABILITIES JOINT & INDIVIDUAL	In Dollars (Omit Cents)
Cash on hand and in banks - Schedule A		Notes payable to banks - Schedule H	
Marketable securities and bonds - Schedule B		Notes payable to others - Schedule H	
Other equities & non-marketable securities - Schedule C		Amounts due on credit cards	
Real Estate owned - Schedule D		Delinquent income tax	
Partial interest in real estate equities - Schedule E		Real estate mortgages payable - Schedule D	
Loans receivable - Schedule F		Delinquent real property taxes	
Automobiles and other personal property		Other debts – itemize:	
Cash value–life insurance - Schedule G			
Vested Pension/Profit Sharing/IRA/KEOGH			
Other assets - itemize:			
		TOTAL OF ALL LIABILITIES	
		NET WORTH (Total All Assets Less Total All Liabilities)	
		TOTAL LIABILITIES AND NET WORTH	
TOTAL ASSETS SOLELY OWNED		INCOME STATEMENT - FOR THE YEAR ENDED 20_____. ATTACH MOST RECENT YEAR'S TAX RETURN	
ASSETS JOINTLY OWNED		ANNUAL INCOME	
Cash on hand and in banks .Schedule A		Salary	
Marketable securities and bonds .Schedule B		Bonus and Commissions	
Other Equities & Non-marketable securities .Schedule C		Interest	
Real Estate owned .Schedule D		Other Income-itemize: (Alimony, child support or separate maintenance income need not be	
Partial interest in real estate equities .Schedule E		revealed if you do not wish to have it considered as a basis for repaying this obligation)	
Loans receivable .Schedule F			
Automobiles and other personal property			
Cash value-life insurance .Schedule G		TOTAL INCOME	
Vested Pension/Profit Sharing/IRA/KEOGH		ANNUAL EXPENSES	
Other assets - itemize:		Home mortgage (principal and interest)	
		Other loan payments	
		Income taxes	
		Property taxes	
		Alimony, child support, separate maintenance	
		Other expenses - itemize:	
TOTAL ASSETS JOINTLY OWNED			
TOTAL OF ALL ASSETS		**TOTAL EXPENSES**	

SCHEDULE A - BANK ACCOUNTS

Name and Location of Bank	Acct. Type	Cash Balance	In Name of

SCHEDULE B - MARKETABLE STOCKS AND BONDS

Number of Shares or Face Value of Bonds	Description	Market Value	In Name of (If Broker, Specify)	Pledged? (Y or N)

SCHEDULE C - OTHER BUSINESS EQUITIES AND NON-MARKETABLE SECURITIES

Number of Shares Or Percentage Interest	Description	In Name Of	Value	Source of Value	Pledged? (Y or N)

SCHEDULE D - REAL ESTATE SOLELY/JOINTLY OWNED

Address and Type of Property Title in name of	% of Ownership	Year Acquired	Cost	Total Market Value	Balance of Mortgage	Value of Partial Equity Owned

The "Oracle of Omaha"

When it comes to the subject of net worth and investing, the most famous person in the world (and one of the richest with a net worth of $50 billion or so) is Warren Buffett who is often referred to as the **Oracle of Omaha.** Ask your friends if they know who the Oracle of Omaha is. I bet they don't. Warren Buffett is from Omaha, Nebraska, and has lived a modest lifestyle in that community for his entire adult life while he pursued his interest in investing. His company is Berkshire Hathaway (stock symbol: BRK/A), of which he is chairman and chief executive officer (CEO) and through which he buys other companies. His company is the largest investor in Coca-Cola, he has a large position in IBM, he recently bought a railroad and many, many other companies.

Believe it or not, at the time I am writing this, the price of just one share of Berkshire Hathaway A stock is $209,000. That's right. $209,000 *per share*. Unbelievable. You should do some research on Warren Buffett and how he decides which stocks and companies he wants to buy. He buys for the long term and does not trade in and out of stocks on a frequent basis as other people do. You can learn a lot from reading about him and watching him interviewed on TV. He has been one of the very best investors of all time.

How much faith does he have in the stock market as the best place to put your money over the long haul? He recently revealed on a television interview that his office manages the pension funds for many of the companies that Berkshire owns (the pensions of thousands of employees) and all the money in those funds are invested in stocks—all of it. Unlike most other pension funds that have a "balanced portfolio" of stocks and bonds, he invests nothing in bonds because, "History has shown us that over time you get better returns on stocks than you do on bonds." When the Oracle of Omaha speaks, people listen and you should, too.

CHAPTER 12

Taxes

(The Lower, the Better)

Remember the Boston Tea Party and "no taxation without representation"? Well … we have had the representation they wanted for a long time, but we have had the taxes for a long time, too. It is a very complicated subject, but bottom line: We all pay taxes to the federal, state, and local governments every year.

Gross Income

Gross income is the total amount of money that you earn in a given year from all sources.

Net Income

Net income is your gross income minus all of the taxes that have to be paid. It is the money you have left over that belongs to you.

Taxes

There is an old saying that there are only two sure things in life: death and taxes. Nobody likes paying taxes, but the truth is that taxes are the main way that our government raises the money it needs to provide the services that we have all come to expect.

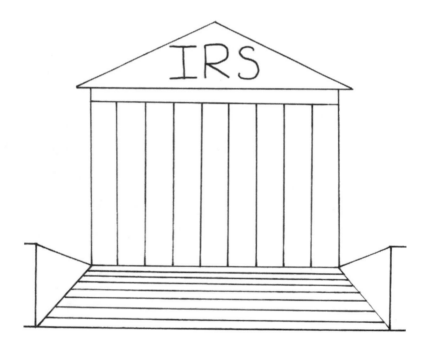

Our military exists because our tax dollars pay for it. We fight terrorism thanks to the tax dollars that employ the people at our spy agencies who keep us safe. Every aspect of government that you can think of is funded, at least in part, with tax dollars: schools, road construction, environmental protection, our criminal and civil justice system, foreign aid, Medicare and Medicaid, the postal system, maintenance of our national parks, NASA, farm support, you name it. It all depends on tax dollars to keep it going.

Taxes are collected by all levels of government: by the federal government in Washington, DC; by the government of each of our 50 states; and even by local cities, municipalities, and taxing districts such as the water authority, the school board, library systems, and so on.

There are all kinds of taxes that we have to pay each year. The most common are income taxes, property taxes, sales taxes, capital gains taxes, Social Security taxes, and taxes on interest and dividends.

It is impossible to describe all of the taxes here; some people spend a lifetime studying our tax code and how it works.

If you took the tax code and all of the tax regulations that accompany it, you could build a pile on your desk several feet high, and each page would be filled with complicated fine print that is difficult to read and understand.

In very simple terms, here are the highlights of the taxes that most people have to pay each year:

Income Taxes

Every year U.S. citizens are required to pay a percentage of their annual income to the federal government as an **income tax.** How much they pay depends on how much they make and what kind of income it was.

Money from a paycheck, also known as ordinary income or personal income, is taxed up to a maximum of about 39.6 percent. But there are taxes added onto that for Medicare and some other things, so the amount you pay in personal income taxes can be even higher. At one point in our history, personal income taxes were as high as 91 percent of one's earned income. Imagine that. People would work hard all year and only ended up keeping 9 percent of what they earned. Fortunately, those days are long gone.

Some states have their own income taxes. If you live in those states, you must pay income taxes to the state in which you live *in addition* to what you pay the U.S. government in federal income taxes. State income taxes are in the range of 5 to 8 percent of your gross income each year.

Florida has no state income tax at all, which is why a lot of people from high-tax states (New York, for example) become Florida residents. If a person earns $1 million per year in New York State, he has to pay 8.82 percent of his income or $88,200 a year to the state of New York in addition to the $400,000 in federal income taxes. A New York resident's combined income tax bill to both the U.S. government and the state of New York: $488,200 (there are ways to reduce your taxes, but we won't get into that now).

If the New York resident moves to Florida, however, and earns $1 million he will *save* up to $88,200 a year because he will not have to pay the New York income tax. As a result, taxes have a big influence on where many people decide to live.

Property Taxes

If you own a house in the United States or other real estate of some kind, you will have to pay property taxes not to the federal government but to the local government where the property is located.

Local government needs money to pay for the local services we require such as fire and police protection, local road repairs, garbage collection, local parks, libraries, street lights, schools, and so on.

In many states property taxes are based on **millage rates,** which is basically a tax rate equal to a certain percentage of the value of the property that you own. On a $1 million house in Coral Gables, Florida for example, you would pay about $11,000 a year in local taxes.

Sales Taxes

Every time we go to the store to buy something or go to a restaurant to have dinner we pay a **sales tax** to the state where the transaction took place. Sales taxes are based on a percentage of what we spend.

In Florida, the sales tax is 6 percent of the purchase price. In other states the sales tax is slightly different but, in general, state sales taxes are usually in the 3 to 7 percent range. The retailer collects the sales tax at the time of the sale (it goes on your credit card if you paid by credit card) and sends the collected tax receipts to the state's tax collector.

Sales taxes are generally considered to be **regressive.** In other words, they end up being a larger percentage of the annual income of a low-income person than they are for a person with a higher income. As a result, many people think sales taxes are unfair and not the best way for a state to raise revenue. That attitude is probably why we do not have a national sales tax, although some people have advocated for one for a long time. In Europe there is a national sales tax, and they call it VAT—value-added tax.

Capital Gains Taxes

A capital gains tax is a tax on the profit that you make on an investment. If you bought a stock and sold it for a profit, you have a **capital gain** and have to pay the capital gains tax. If you bought a commercial building and sold it for a profit, you have a capital gain and have to pay the capital gains tax. There are many other examples of capital gains that would require you to pay this tax.

There are two kinds of capital gains taxes: **long term** and **short term.** The magic cutoff between the two is whether you owned your investment for more or less than one year.

If you own a stock for more than one year and sell it for a profit, you have to pay the long-term capital gains tax of 20 percent of your profit. If you owned the stock for less than one year and sold it for a profit, you would have to pay the short–term capital gains tax of up to 39.6 percent of your profit.

Assume for the moment that you bought 100 shares of Apple stock at $525/share and sold the shares two years later for $625/share. What would your tax be?

Since you owned the stock for more than one year, you would pay the long-term capital gains rate of 20 percent. Your profit here was $100 per share or $10,000. As a result your capital gains tax would be $2,000.

If you owned the stock for less than one year, you would pay the short-term capital gains rate of up to 39.6 percent or $3,960 in this example.

Many people will not sell a stock until they have owned it for at least a year so that they can take advantage of the lower long-term capital gains rate.

Social Security Taxes

In 1935 President Franklin Delano Roosevelt signed into law our nation's first **Social Security** law as part of his New Deal for America. The law was designed to assist the elderly in their retirement by providing them with a monthly check so that they would have some minimum income in order to live.

Social Security is a very complicated program, and I cannot possibly explain it all here. But for now at least, all you need to know is that everyone who gets a paycheck during their working years pays a Social Security tax to the government. The tax is in addition to the federal income tax that everyone has to pay.

When you are 62, you are eligible to start receiving Social Security payments from the government, and you can spend the money any way you want to. You paid into the system when you were young, and you get to start taking money out of the system when you are older.

Taxes on Interest Income

If you have money in a savings account at the bank, you will be paid interest on the money each year. If you own bonds you will be paid interest on the bonds you own. If you lend money to someone, you may be paid interest on the money you lent. These are just a few examples of how people earn **interest income.**

Interest is taxed by the federal government at ordinary income tax rates, which can go up to about 39.6 percent.

Taxes on Dividends

Dividends are trickier. They can be taxed at ordinary income tax rates or at capital gains rates depending on whether or not they are qualified dividends. You will need to speak to your accountant about this when the need arises.

Audits

Audits are a simple term to understand. An audit is when an outside accountant comes in to review the financial records of a company to make sure that they are being kept according to **generally accepted accounting practices (GAAP)** and to make sure there was no fraud or other financial irregularity occurring at the company.

Most companies have their own internal accounting or bookkeeping departments whose job it is to maintain the daily records of how much money is coming in to the company, bill payment, payroll matters, cash management, and so on. Problems can occur, however, when the people who work in that department are either incompetent or, worse, when they try to quietly steal money from the company.

To make sure that the financial books and records are accurate, companies will hire outside accounting firms to come in once a year and review everything. When the outside review is completed, the independent auditors will issue a report on whether everything is okay or whether they found any problems. Unless a company has **audited financial statements,** you can never be sure that the financial information you are receiving from a company is totally accurate.

The Internal Revenue Service (IRS) of the federal government also conducts audits of individuals and companies in the United States. Each year the IRS will select certain taxpayers and audit their previously filed tax returns to make sure that they were accurate and the full amount of the annual taxes that were owed were paid. If mistakes were made or fraud was committed penalties can be imposed or an offending taxpayer can be sent to jail. Never cheat on your taxes. You will sleep better at night.

CHAPTER 13

The Economy

(The Business of Business)

It's not just about picking good stocks. To be a good investor you also have to understand what is going on with the overall economy because all businesses are interdependent. Your stocks are not likely to do well if other businesses are doing poorly. Here are some things to look at to get a sense for how the economy is doing.

The Federal Reserve (The Fed)

To have some basic understanding of the U.S. financial system, you need to at least know that there is this thing called the **Federal Reserve,** more commonly known as the **Fed.** It is an agency of the U.S. government. It reports to Congress but is independent of the executive, legislative, and judicial branches of our government.

The Fed is the central bank for our country, the top dog, the main man, the king of banking and money in the United States. Currently, the chairperson of the Fed is **Janet Yellen.** She is the first woman ever to head the Federal Reserve.

The Fed was created by Congress in 1913 to help stabilize our financial system after a series of financial crises. The Great Depression in 1929 resulted in even further powers being granted to the Fed as the United States struggled to get control over an economy that was weak and facing collapse.

Countless books have been written about the Fed. Colleges teach courses on the Fed and its role in our economy, and you could spend years studying its history and the impact of its actions. All that will be for later in your life. For right now, however, all you need to know are the very basics.

Congress established the Fed so that it would enact monetary policies that:

1. Maximize employment
2. Stabilize prices
3. Maintain moderate long-term interest rates
4. Regulate monetary policy
5. Regulate banks
6. Provide financial services to banks
7. Publish economic research like the **beige book**

Think about it. From the standpoint of our country as a whole (a macroeconomic perspective), all these objectives for the Fed are good things. They are laudable goals that every country and economy should aspire to achieve in order to thrive and be successful.

Don't we want moderate interest rates? Don't we want to maximize employment? Don't we want our banks regulated so that they don't collapse with our money in them and damage our economy? One would think so. Right?

But even the Fed has its detractors. There are well-known politicians in Washington, DC, who think the Fed is unnecessary and we should get rid of it. Despite the debate, however, the Fed is here to stay.

Think of the Fed as a watchdog for our economy and banking system. It is composed of a lot of really smart economists and financial experts who are constantly monitoring what is going on with interest rates, our economy, and our banks.

If the Fed sees that things are good—if we have low unemployment, if businesses are doing well and making money, if banks are financially stable and lending money to businesses and families—then the Fed won't need to intervene. If, on the other hand, unemployment is high, interest rates are spiking, and banks are not lending money to keep our economy moving, then the Fed has the economic tools to help fix that.

Enough said about the Fed for the time being. This is really a subject matter that requires much more study, but for now at least you know a little something about it.

Gross—As in Really Gross—Domestic Product (GDP)

Why would anything be called **gross** when it comes to money? An old sandwich that you find in the bottom of your backpack is gross, a dead mouse under your sink is gross, but what's the story with gross as we use the term here? Just what is gross domestic product, and what makes it gross?

Gross Domestic Product (GDP) is the value of all of
the finished goods and services that the United States pro-
duces in the course of a year. Think about it. If you added up
the value of every single finished product manufactured in the
United States in one year and added to it the value of all the
services rendered by people in the service industry (waiters
and waitresses, hotel clerks, teachers, police, firemen, doctors, lawyers, etc.) who work in our country, the grand total
for all of that would be our country's GDP or gross domestic
product.

How big or gross is our GDP? In 2012 the value of all
finished goods and services produced by the U.S. economy

was $16 trillion. That's right: trillion, not billion. Here is what the number looks like:

$16,000,000,000,000

This is a piece of trivia you can use the next time you have lunch at school. Ask your friends if they have any idea what the GDP was for the United States last year, and see what they say. My guess is they will not even come close.

Why is GDP important, and why should you know something about it? A couple of reasons. First, it is a term you will hear discussed on the financial news programs, and the next time you hear about it or read about it, you will know what people are talking about. Second, investors need to know whether the GDP of our country is growing and getting bigger each year or whether it is contracting and we are producing less than what we produced the year before.

A growing economy is usually good for the stock market. As companies make and sell more goods, they will make more money and hopefully generate more profits. Increasing profits drive increases in stock prices. Remember the **price/earnings (P/E) ratio?**

GDP calculations, however, only look backward. In other words, by the time economists calculate what the GDP was for any given quarter or any given year, that time period has already come and gone and we are looking at a number for how things were in the past, not how they are at this moment.

That's the problem with looking at historical data. Nevertheless, it is helpful to know what the GDP numbers show. They are yet another data point in helping us understand whether we are in a **contracting economy,** a **stagnant economy,** or a **growing economy.** Understanding the big picture, or **macroeconomics,** as economists like to say, can help us make a forecast about future economic performance not just for the economy as a whole but for any company we may be considering buying stock in.

Anyone who buys stocks or makes other investments is really making a bet on future economic performance. When you buy shares of Apple, you are not buying the stock because the company made a lot of money last year. You are buying the stock because you believe it will make a lot of money this year or next year or the year after that. Part of your analysis is knowing whether we are in an economy that will support increasing spending by Apple customers, and to have some insight about that you need to pay attention to GDP.

The other reason why this matters is because Wall Street's forecast for whether GDP is expected to grow by 1 percent or 4 percent has a direct impact on stock prices. If the big players on Wall Street believe that GDP growth is accelerating, they may be more likely to bid up the price of stocks. If, on the other hand, they believe that GDP growth is expected to be weak, then they will not be as willing to pay more for stocks, and that will directly impact the value of the stocks that you own or are considering buying in the future. For all these reasons, you need to pay attention to the popular consensus for GDP growth.

Budgets

A **budget** is a plan or a **forecast** of the money you expect to earn or collect in the future along with a list of the expenses you expect to incur over the same period of time.

Every year the president of the United States submits a budget to Congress that projects in great detail what our nation's sources of revenue are expected to be for the coming year and how the federal government will spend the money it takes in. Conceptually, it is no different than the budget that the average American family makes for itself.

BUDGET

Income

- salary
- interest
- dividends

Expenses

- mortgage payment
- car payment
- insurance

Families have to have some idea of how much money they expect to earn each year so that they can be sure to *live within their means*. That process of planning for anticipated income and expenses is called **budgeting.** A budget is simply a side-by-side allocation of the money you expect to receive over a given period of time and the money you expect to spend over the same period of time.

Budgets in Action

There are three kinds of budgets that you can have:

1. **Budget deficit.** If you prepare a budget that shows that you will be spending more than you expect to earn, you are projecting a budget deficit.
2. **Budget surplus.** If your budget shows that you will be earning more than you are forecasting to spend, you are projecting a budget surplus.
3. **Balanced budget.** If your budget indicates that you will be spending exactly what you expect to earn, you have what is called a balanced budget.

These days everyone is focused on budget deficits for our federal government because we have been spending more than we have been collecting in taxes. Our country has not seen a budget surplus in many years.

Our National Debt

The U.S. government has been spending more money than it takes in for a long time, and to pay for all of our excessive spending, we have been borrowing money from everyone who buys U.S. Treasury notes and bonds. (Remember our discussion about Treasuries and all of the money we have been borrowing from the Chinese?)

Over the years we have borrowed and borrowed and borrowed to the point that we have now racked up an indescribably gigantic mountain of debt. How much debt do we now have outstanding and unpaid? Are you ready for the answer?

Are you ready to be shocked beyond belief? $17.5 trillion! That's right. Not billion—trillion! A total of $17.5 trillion of **debt.** It is such a big number you can't even comprehend it and, as you may remember, it is almost exactly what the value is of our GDP for one year. Remember that $16 trillion number?

If you want to understand just how big our national debt is, go to **www.usdebtclock.org.** You won't believe the numbers. The numbers are stunning, and they are changing by the second as you watch the site. Check it out.

Deficits and the National Debt; So What? What Do They Have to Do with Investing?

Do deficits and our national debt actually matter to someone who is interested in the stock market? Should these issues even be considered in deciding what stocks to buy? The answer is: Yes.

If, for example, you were considering an investment in companies that depend on doing business with the federal government and, because we are spending too much money on paying interest on our national debt, Congress will soon reduce spending on military hardware (fighter jets, warships, new weapons systems, and futuristic new technologies), then you may decide not to buy stock in Lockheed Martin, General Dynamics, Raytheon, and other companies that do a lot of business with our military.

All companies have a better chance of prospering in a robust economy where the outlook for future business is good and we are not overburdened by debt. As you would expect, the stock market would respond positively to that as well.

Bull markets (a favorite for people who buy stocks) are more likely when government spending can support companies in the United States rather than diverting our spending to pay interest to our bondholders in China and other foreign countries.

You should always keep an eye on our national debt and the burden of making the interest payments on that debt. It is an important component of the overall economy and has a direct impact on the taxes we pay and the general health of our economy.

CHAPTER 14

Venture Capital and Private Equity

(Big Bets Chasing Big Profits)

Venture capitalists and private equity investors frequently invest directly in private companies where there is no public market for the stock and the only way to monetize their investments (which is a fancy way of saying "make money") is to make sure the companies they invest in are successful.

Venture Capital (VC)

Venture capital refers to money raised from wealthy people that is then invested in various young companies in the hope that the investors will earn huge returns on their money; much greater than if the money had simply been invested in regular stocks or bonds.

Investing is all about *risk and reward*. If you buy a stock, you take a risk that the price could fall and you lose some money. If you want a guaranteed return of 3 percent, you can buy a U.S. **Treasury bond** and have no risk at all. But if you want the possibility of a huge return—10 times what you invested, 20 times what you invested, or even more—then you can consider becoming a venture capitalist or investing in a venture capital fund. Always remember, however, that if you want the possibility of huge returns, you have to be willing to take huge risks. You can easily lose 100 percent of your money with a venture capital investment, so be careful.

There are hundreds of venture capital firms around the world, and they are all out there looking for the next Google or Apple or Facebook and hoping to score big.

Kleiner Perkins and **Sequoia** are two of the biggest and most established VC firms. They have been doing business for nearly 50 years and have invested in hundreds of young companies that went on to become very successful. In the process their founders have made a fortune. You can read more about these two venture capital firms on their websites.

Unlike mutual funds, which take money from investors and then use the money to buy stocks and bonds that are traded on the stock market, venture capital funds take in investor money and then frequently use it to invest in private companies that they get actively involved in helping to manage. To be sure, they will invest in public companies as well but their investments in private companies present more of a challenge in terms of getting a return on their money because the private company investments are harder to sell then the stock of a public company investment.

Stocks of public companies purchased by the average small investor are a **passive** investment and require no active management. When you buy stocks, you rely on other people to run the companies. With venture capital, however, the VC firms will typically take a seat on the company's board of directors and spend considerable time monitoring and advising the companies that they invest in. It is a real hands-on, **active** investment for them.

The companies that VCs invest in are usually young or **early stage** that may have just a few employees and need money to grow. They may have previously taken in some **seed money** from friends and family, but they lack the money and the expertise to really take the company to the next level. For that, they need seasoned investors with the money and the experience to help the company move ahead, and that is where venture capital firms come in. They bring not only money to the companies they invest in but managerial expertise as well.

If a venture fund is interested in possibly investing in a company, it will send a team of people to meet with the company's management and learn everything there is to know about it. That process of investigating the company before investing is known as **due diligence**.

"Due Diligence" is like homework. The more you do, the more you know the subject matter.

When the VC's diligence team completes its work, it will make a recommendation to the board of the VC firm about whether to invest or not invest in the young company. If they decide to invest, they will make the company an **offer** detailing how much they are willing to invest and on what terms. The offer they make is presented in a **term sheet**, which is usually just a few pages long. If the company finds the terms acceptable, a **contract** will then be signed and the VC's investment into the company will be made.

If the company rejects the VC's terms, that is the end of it. The VC firm will move on to another deal, and the young company will have to find the money and expertise it needs to grow elsewhere.

Many young companies often find the investment terms offered by VC firms onerous. The VCs usually want to value the young company at less than what the founders think it is worth; they want to own a much greater percentage of the company in exchange for their investment than the founders are prepared to give them; they typically want more control over how the company is run than the company is comfortable with, and they will insist on seats on the board of directors as well. For young, struggling companies, although they may not like the proposed terms, if they need the money they will have no choice but to agree to what the VCs are offering.

Companies that got their start as a result of venture capital investments include Amazon, Facebook, Groupon, Twitter, Google, Netscape, WebMD, AOL, Apple, YouTube, PayPal, Yahoo!, WhatsApp, LinkedIn, and Genentech.

These were all the venture capital winners, but there were plenty of losers as well. VCs are not right 100 percent of the time; far from it. Some of their investments turn out to be bad deals and they lose their money, but their objective is to be right more often than they are wrong.

When VCs invest it is basically an **educated bet** that the young company will do well and, with a lot of hard work, after the investment is made they hope to earn a big return on their money.

The history of venture capital in the United States is the history of the new economy in our country. The computer industry, social media, and the birth of Internet businesses all owe their existence to the willingness of venture capitalists to make the investments in those businesses when no one else would. It is a fascinating industry.

There are many books written about the venture capital industry, and if you are interested, you should read some of them.

Private Equity

Private equity is similar to venture capital in the sense that it is money from private investors who inject working capital into an existing business in exchange for stock, but private equity investors tend to invest in more mature companies that have a real business and may very well already be making money. Venture capitalists usually invest in much younger start-up companies that are just getting going and may have no product, no earnings, and no market presence at all.

Private equity investors are more risk averse than VCs, and the business model they use for deals is very different from the venture capital model.

CHAPTER 15

Money Smart

(Move to the Front of the Class!)

Congratulations! If you made it this far, you are on your way. You are now smarter than you were before you read this book and know more about money, investing, and the stock market than most people your age. Never stop learning about all of this. You will need these skills for the rest of your life.

Retirement Savings

Retirement simply refers to the day when you stop working, which you can do only if you have saved enough money to support your lifestyle or if you will continue to have an income of some sort after you retire. One way or the other, you have to pay your bills after you are done working. When you are a kid, retirement may seem so far away that it is not even worth thinking about, but it is a concept that you need to know something about even at a young age.

Most people graduate from high school in their late teens. They graduate from college around the age of 22, and some then go on to graduate school for another two to five years. Law school, for example, is another three years after college. Medical school is maybe five more years after college. Getting a master's in business administration (MBA) is another two years after college, and so on.

Once you are out of school, you will start your working career, and if all goes well, you will make enough money to start saving for the day when you decide to stop working and retire. People retire at different ages, but generally speaking, retirement age is usually somewhere between 60 and 75.

Some people never retire. They keep working either because they have not saved enough money to support their lifestyle or because they love it and that is how they want to spend their time.

What you want to do in life is *give yourself the ability to retire if you want to,* and for that, you need to have your finances in order and a plan in place to make it happen.

At the moment, there is a U.S. government program called **Social Security,** which was started back in 1935 as part of President Franklin Delano Roosevelt's New Deal following the Great Depression. It provides monthly checks to people who are 62 or older, but the checks are not big; maybe $2,200 per month or so. It is paid for through a payroll tax that all workers pay whenever they get a paycheck.

Young people today, however, cannot count on Social Security to be there for them when they retire. For many years the Social Security program has been paying out more money than it has been taking in. As a result, if something is not done to fix it, the day will come when it is broke and it will no longer be able to pay out what is needed to keep it going.

A person of your age should just assume that Social Security as we know it now will not be there to help support you in your retirement. In order to retire, if that is what you want to do, you will need to save enough money on your own so that you can support yourself without government assistance.

There are various ways to make sure you have money when the day comes that you want to stop working. There are different kinds of **pension plans** that you can pay into during your career; there are **insurance policies** and **annuities** that you can buy that will pay out money to you when you retire; or you can simply save your money, invest it wisely, and build up an account that you can draw from to support you later in life.

The thing you need to remember regarding all of this, however, is that you will need to plan for retirement on your own and there is no magic way to make it happen. When it is all said and done, it takes money. There is no getting around that. It will be up to you to have saved enough money and structured your investments so that you will have the cash flow you need to pay for your lifestyle when you are done working.

Keep all of this in mind when your career begins; always make sure to save some of what you earn, and do not allow your lifestyle to cost more to maintain than you can afford. *Remember the number 1 rule: Live within your means!* By the time you are ready to retire you will look back and be very grateful that you thought about this early in life.

It is *never* too early to start saving money and thinking ahead.

Your Mission, Should You Choose to Accept It

Kids of your generation have a big job to take on. You are inheriting a super huge national debt, and it will be up to you and everyone else your age to be smart about how to deal with it. How do you pay all of the interest on that debt? How do you reduce the debt burden? Will it ever be possible to pay it all off? Is it smart to even try to pay it all off?

These are just some of the questions that you and your peers will have to wrestle with as you get older, and that is why the subjects in this book are so important. They will get you thinking about the important topics of your day and help you and the best and the brightest of your age plan for the moment when you will take charge. That day will be here before you know it. Embrace it. Seize the opportunity. *It will be your moment to shine.*

You Are Now Money Smart!

Congratulations! You made it! It was a whirlwind tour of the basic topics of money, investing, and the stock market.

If you read this book from start to finish, you obviously have what it takes to learn about these important topics and to become money smart.

Think about what you have learned; use this book as a guide whenever you have a question about one of the topics, and study the topics in more detail as often as possible.

You are now *way ahead* of other kids your age, and you are on the road to success.

Keep up the good work!

CHAPTER 16

AND SO IT ENDS—OR MAYBE THIS IS JUST THE BEGINNING

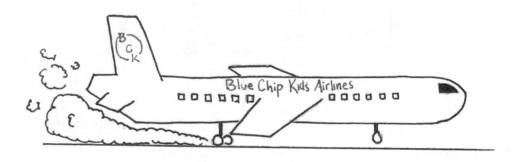

"Attention passengers, the captain has indicated that we will be landing shortly. Please make sure that your seat belts are buckled and your seatbacks and tray tables are in the upright and locked positions. Thank you for flying with us. We hope you enjoyed the journey and we hope to see you again soon on Blue Chip Kids airline."

What a trip. We have traveled to a lot of interesting and important places since our journey began. The point of this book was not to make you an expert in anything but to intro-duce you to the world of money, investing, and the stock market so that you will be interested enough to want to learn more about them.

If you take the time to read this book a few times and to think about what you are reading, you will have a better appreciation for what it takes to earn money, manage money, and plan for your financial future. No one will do this for you. You have to do it yourself, and you have the intelligence and the commitment to make it happen.

Good luck. And stay tuned. The "Blue Chip Kids" are getting ready for their next exciting journey.

DISCLAIMER

To keep the lawyers happy, let me be clear: You should not spend or invest your money or your parents' money without first consulting with people who know what they are doing. The information in this book was intended to introduce you to basic concepts about money, investing, and the stock market and should not be used as the basis for making investments until you learn more about what you are doing.

ABOUT THE AUTHOR

This book started as a simple idea to write a few pages for our 13-year-old son Trent so that he could learn something about money, investing, and the stock market. Despite the fact that he goes to a very good school, they do not teach anything about these subjects in middle school, and it is not part of the curriculum once he enters high school. In my opinion, the subject matter is just too important to ignore, so I decided to take on the teaching responsibility myself. The end result is this book with 100 topics and 165 kid-friendly illustrations. Originally intended only for our son, I eventually agreed to make it available to anyone who might be interested in reading it.

We have got to wake up in this country and get serious about teaching kids about financial matters. The skills necessary to earn, manage, and invest one's money should be just as important as geology, astronomy, art, frog dissection, algebra, playing a musical instrument, soccer, and yes, even football.

There is now plenty of research demonstrating that our high school graduates rank behind students from many other countries when it comes to an understanding of financial matters, and additional research shows that if they are taught these skills before they graduate, they will make better financial decisions later in life.

Crushing student debt holds back too many young people from realizing their dreams. Senior citizens are having their Social Security payments reduced to pay off school debt from years ago. There is an immediate need to educate people about how to manage and invest money and the burdens brought on by too much debt. As parents we need to act, and this book is the start of my commitment to do something about this problem. More in the *Blue Chip* Kids series is in the works.

In my real life, I am a lawyer with the law firm of Stewart Tilghman Fox Bianchi & Cain, PA in Miami, Florida, where I have practiced law for 35 years. I graduated magna cum laude from Tufts University with a BA in economics and earned my law degree at Boston College Law School. A complete copy of my biography can be found at http://www.stfblaw.com/attorneys/david-bianchi/.

INDEX